OTHER BOOKS BY JAN MARQUART

Write to Heal
The Mindful Writer, Still the Mind, Free the Pe
The Basket Weaver, a Novel
Kate's Way, a Novel
Echoes from the Womb, a Book for Daughters
Voices from the Land
The Breath of Dawn, a Journey of Everyday Blessings
How to Write from Your Heart (booklet)
How to Write Your Own Memoir (booklet)
A Manual on How to Deal with a Bully in the Workplace
A Writer's Wisdom
Unveil the Wounded Self, a Guided Journal for PTSD Sufferers
Never Too Late, a Novel
Cracked Open, a Book of Poems
Light, a Book of Poems
Eternal, a Book of Poems
Still, Haiku
Leaves Clapping, a Book of Poetry

CHILDREN'S BOOKS

Can You Find My Love? (Book series also available in Spanish)

Book 1: Seasons
Book 2: Things to Do Outside
Book 3: Why We Need Rain
Book 4: Things with Wheels
Book 5: Families (English only)

Book 6: Bugs
Book 7: In the Sea
Book 8: Morning
Book 9: On Your Head
Book 10: Babies

"If one can capture the profoundly enigmatic, epic, and enduring relationship between daughter and mother, Jan Marquart has found the way, entering and chronicling this labyrinth with reminiscences both tender and raw. The complexity of love co-mingled with parental control, and the ebb and flow of motherly affection and disaffection weaves its way through Jan's testimonial to this most formative of dyads. Women born to strong materfamilias will find resemblance and resonance in this exceptionally moving memoir."

—SUSAN HUTCHINSON, poet, educator, and author of *1st Class Travel to Tanzania* and *Global Odysseys of Minkey and Winkey*

"Jan Marquart's *Lunch with Mom: a Daughter's Soliloquy*, is a spellbinding tale of the author's life, starting with her earliest memories as a child playing with her friends in Brooklyn. She remembers her mother breathing poems into the air, but mothers are not perfect, and Marquart doesn't hold back. This book is written as a soliloquy to her mother, speaking the truth, the truth that her parents really didn't want to hear. This memoir is a 'hold on to your hats!' journey of perseverance and healing."

—BECKY VENTURA, author of *Radiant Jukebox* and *Quintessential Cubicles*

"This account of a life fully led certainly leaves no stone unturned, which makes for a powerful read indeed. An extraordinary amount of care and sensitivity has been bravely invested by Jan Marquart in telling this, her life story, so openly, displaying such a knowing and mature level of reflection throughout. These very qualities make me supremely confident that Lunch with Mom: a Daughter's Soliloquy will prove to be valuable to all those who choose to read it."

—Scott Hastie, author of *Timeless* and *Splinters of Light*

"Jan Marquart triumphs in her exploration of the complex relationship between mothers and daughters and intimately reveals how her relationship with her mother impacted her life."

—LESLIE WEBSTER, poet, YA author, and educator

"Jan Marquart's tale will resonate with many mothers and daughters alike. She bravely confronts the reality of the love and the fury that often accompanies that relationship."

—KAY CORDTZ, author of *A Murder in Old Town*

LUNCH
with
M◯M

A Daughter's Soliloquy

JAN MARQUART

Printed in the United States of America.
Produced by Publish Pros | publishpros.com

ISBN: 979-8-9914361-0-6

This work depicts actual events in the life of the author as truthfully as recollection permits. While all persons within are actual individuals, some names and identifying characteristics have been omitted or changed to respect their privacy. This narrative is not intended to expose anyone to harm, or unduly speak about them.

I dedicate this book to all daughters. May the path of being a daughter allow you to find the sound of your own voice and purpose. And in all the confusion of life, I hope you find appreciation for whatever your mother's contribution to your life was. Sometimes our mothers abandon us. Sometimes our mothers give us support.

Whatever your mother did or did not give you, it was the foundation for your own being. For that reason, daughters and mothers will never be fully separate. Both are sacred.

Make a cup of tea

Sit

Breathe in

Breathe out

Breathe in

Breathe out

Breathe in

Breathe out

Turn the page.

SCREAMS

I was born through my mother's screams
as I freed myself from her womb
screams that echoed throughout my life
I am my mother's daughter
and her mother's granddaughter
and her mother's great-granddaughter
we are one long string of paper dolls

Oh, the thin ice daughters travel.

And, the anger we stir.
Wanting what no woman should want
To give in to inexhaustive curiosity
To live from our hearts
Our inner knowing
To live a life dictated by the spirit within.

My mother's screams were loud
Her silent screams deadly

The lesson girls learn:
Please others
At our own sacrifice.

My ambitious journey to the self
Kept her screams in the wind.

THE BEGINNING

Hi, Mom. There were many conversations we did not have, so I am speaking to you now as my life has entered its winter season.

I imagine we are sitting across from one another at our favorite lunch spot, The Green Tea Room on 86th Street, after returning from shopping at A&S. Our arms heavy with shopping bags, exhaustion showing on both our faces.

Let's order our usual: grilled cheese sandwiches, French fries and Cokes. And we can remember our overstuffed shopping bags pushed under the table and snuggled close beside us on those ugly and often sticky red plastic booths.

So, here I sit, at seventy-four, writing to you from my heart, without anger or displeasure or disappointment. I am the historian of my life, but together we are historians of our relationship.

And because now, I have ripened, it is time.

* * *

I'm going to start my story, Mom, going back as far as I can remember. It is amazing to me how much I remember, and you often said you were stunned at my memory. I know many people who can't remember their childhoods at all. In this light, we are so alike. Your stories of your childhood were prolific, and I learned so much about your life listening to you at our Formica kitchen table. I think I know about fifty percent of your childhood.

Now, I want to tell you about my life, the life I haven't shared with you before for a multitude of reasons. It is important that I do so not just to rehash my life but, in an effort, to attempt to understand us. You are the one who taught me how to be a girl, teen, young woman. Isn't it our mothers who teach us the foundation of becoming a woman? If not you, then who? I hear many women attributing their development and success in feeling loved and becoming who they are to their grandmothers or aunts because their mothers abandoned them or died. But even that, even living without a mother is critical in how daughters develop. Absence is just as powerful as presence. I'll spare you all my memories, Mom. Some I've already told you. But I have, at this point in my life, a need to share more and to try to understand more. So here is my first memory.

I was standing up in my pink crib holding onto the bars. I heard you walk towards my bedroom and I felt happy. I started jumping up and down. You appeared in the doorway, your brown hair curled over your shoulders.

"Oh, Janet!" you yelled.

I stopped bouncing and fixed my eyes on you. I went numb and became frightened. Then you were on your knees, your hair bouncing as you washed the pink bars of my crib with a rag up and down. You were upset with me and your voice was angry. I was confused. I had no idea what was happening. I watched you put your hand into a bucket of water to rinse the rag then wipe the bars again. I made you unhappy and I felt changed. I can still feel that moment, Mom. How young could I have been, standing in a crib in diapers? Did I cry then, Mom? I don't remember crying. I can only say I stopped jumping up and down, no longer feeling happy. I was having fun before you entered the room, and I was joyful you were coming near me, when suddenly everything stopped and the joy was gone.

Do you remember that day? Could it be the chasm between us started that early in my lifetime? Could that have been the seed for why I held myself responsible for your happiness? Could that have been why, from then on, I did what you said and gave up speaking honestly to you when I disagreed? I think about these things because even though you have been gone for decades now and I am an elderly woman, I still think about the experiences we had together.

Here is another young memory, Mom. I was a toddler the day you came into my room and told me you named me after your favorite doll because you loved the name Janet. Your voice became excited as you spoke of your favorite doll. Your eyes lit up. I wanted to be excited too, but I wasn't. I was mad. I didn't want the same name as your stupid doll. I wanted my own name. I wanted to tell you this, but I was afraid you wouldn't like it, or maybe I was afraid you wouldn't like me. I adored you. I wanted to know you adored me too. I scrutinized you. I wanted to be like you. You were beautiful. You knew how to do everything.

Remember when you bought me a bag of paper plates the day I stayed home from kindergarten with a cold, and you told me to draw a different face on each plate? I wondered how you could think of such a fun idea. And the time you showed me how to use the edge of open scissors to curl ribbon. You seemed to know how to do awesome and amazing things. You were creative and could make, crochet, sew, cook, and design so many things. That's how I wanted to be. In fact, that is still how I want to be. I love being creative and I owe that to you.

In kindergarten, my teacher had the most wonderful butterscotch-colored high heels. One day you left your closet door open, and I saw you had a pair of butterscotch-colored heels too. I slid my tiny feet into their toes and clonked around the living room, my tiny feet barely remaining in the toes. I heard you call from the kitchen to take the shoes off or I was going to break my neck. It was exciting to walk in your shoes, to pretend I was you, to feel my feet against the toe of the shoe that held your feet. I refused to take the shoes off. Remember? I think you eventually hid them from me, because one day I couldn't find them.

You always had the prettiest nails. Of all the moms in the neighborhood, you had the prettiest. You polished them watching TV and I enthusiastically put my tiny fingers on the TV tray next to your long slim ones, asking you to polish my nails too. I wanted my fingers to look sleek and pretty like yours. To me you were magic. Maybe that is how little girls view their mothers no matter who they are, but I'm sure you were extra special.

Remember the time I came home from first grade and my assignment was to write a poem? I had no idea how to write one. I sat next to you on the couch and asked for help. You looked up at the ceiling and, as if the words were simply hanging in the air, you spoke a poem—just like that. You were awesome. How did you do that so easily? Here is my poem now, Mom.

I fell in love with the moon inside you
as it lit the rooms with your smile
as your breath wrote poems in the air
sending them up to the sky
my heart
a magnifying glass
examining you from all angles
where my own dreams became
a wind embracing the mountains.

I examined everything you did and the way you did it so I could do the same and be like you. I was in a garden waiting to be planted. You were my rock, my fertile soil, my seed. Daughters can't think that way too long or they won't have their own lives. But we certainly don't see admiring our mothers as potentially dangerous for our own souls.

I waited to hear that you thought the same about me. That you thought I was awesome and perfect, beautiful and creative, but I never heard it. I wanted to hear how proud you were of me, but I never heard that either. Maybe, in some crazy way, not hearing those reassurances made me tougher. Back then, telling kids how wonderful they were was viewed as spoiling them, but I didn't think being spoiled was so bad. And I certainly didn't agree that spoiling me would make me selfish.

Daughters worry about mothers just as mothers worry about daughters. For instance, when I was three-and-a-half, I remember being at Grandma's. I was playing in the middle of the room. You told me you were going out for butter, but you didn't come back. I looked out the window into the dark night. I began crying and asked Grandma where you were because I was afraid something was wrong. I told her you always came back after going to the store. She took me in her arms and pulled me tightly to her big bosom and rocked me with force trying to calm me, but there was no calming me.

The next day Dad drove me in his black Ford—the car with the steps that pulled out so passengers didn't have to jump to the ground—to a building about six stories high. There you were, standing in the window, wearing the shimmering tangerine robe Nana had made for you. The next thing I remember, Dad, Poppy, Grandma, you, and me were in the car coming back from the hospital. Grandma had a little baby on her lap and was telling her she had chicken legs. Then she looked at me and told me after I was born I had chicken legs too. Poppy sat in the front seat with Dad, Grandma sat next to me, and you were there on my right. Dad parked the car, and we all headed for the vestibule. I couldn't stop begging you to let me hold her, and you said I could, but only if I sat all the way back on the couch. Then you gently put the baby in my arms, and I thought she was a miracle.

I told you this story when I was thirteen and we were in the kitchen. You were shocked at the details I remembered, especially how excited I was to hold the baby, my new baby sister.

But something strange happened after that. Each time you went to the grocery store, I sat on the edge of the stoop waiting for you to turn up the street with all your bags of groceries. I didn't realize why I felt anxious when you walked out the door to go grocery shopping until I put the pieces together through journal writing many decades later. I'm only telling you this now to remind you that daughters worry about something happening to their mothers just as mothers worry something might happen to their daughters. I guess that's what mothers and daughters do for each other, Mom, always wanting the other to be safe. Always yearning for closeness, and never quite knowing how or why their closeness became a moat. But this next memory might further explain that.

One day, at the age of about five, Dad was playing with my baby sister on the living room floor. She had to have been a little over one. He told me to go help you in the kitchen. I didn't want to, but he insisted because I was the big girl now and had to help you. I went into the kitchen. You were washing dishes. You handed me a dish and showed me how to dry it with the towel. As I was waiting for the next dish, I had a strong urge to wrap my arms around your thigh and tell you how much I loved you. But I hesitated and looked up at you, thinking, *I can't touch Mom, she won't like it.* That moment, standing in front of our white porcelain sink, I knew a life-changing enlightenment had just been made. Even at five, I knew it was an impactful moment. I felt it hit my gut hard. You became an island. That moment not only hurt, it swallowed me.

Please don't get me wrong, Mom, you were a conscientious mom, always trying to make sure my life was full of wholesome activities, always thinking ahead of what I might need. I was grateful you were trying to help me even though I started to feel some separation between what you wanted for me and what I wanted for myself. I wanted to play the flute; you wanted me to play the piano because you always wanted to take lessons, but Grandma couldn't afford it for you. So, you saved and saved and bought me a piano and gave me expensive lessons. I hated the piano. Instead of feeling heard, I felt misunderstood because my opposition to your sacrifice meant I was ungrateful. But I'm getting a little ahead of myself.

You were my first language. I am not writing this to argue, condemn, or prove anything. I simply want to open the space between us so I can tell you about your daughter, the daughter you might not have realized you had.

I miss our lunches at The Green Tea Room. Over the years that small diner was one place we shared our exhaustion over shopping and enjoyed our lunch together, ordering the same thing and forgetting our differences.

This next poem is to give you my account of childhood memories. I hope you enjoy it. Then I want to tell you about another part of my life that I had only because of you.

FROM

I am from parents who survived rough childhoods, who learned the power of respect,

I am from "children should be seen and not heard,"

I am from a roof over my head, good food on the table, decent clothes on my back, no standing on beds or tables,

I am from saddle shoes and loafers polished to perfection,

I am from Wagon Train, Maverick, Amos and Andy, Lawrence Welk, and Perry Como,

I am from playing in the shade of parked cars,

I am from home-cooked meals, food bought in mom-and-pop grocery stores, butchers who knew the cut of meat you liked and called you by your first name,

I am from buying a slice as you walked 5th Avenue to shop, meet friends and neighbors, get caught up on gossip,

I am from learning to ride a bike on Shore Road with the Statue of Liberty watching from behind me, the Hudson glistening,

I am from learning to swim in warm water at Coney Island,

I am from lobster dinners on Friday nights at Lundy's at Sheepshead Bay while divers dove for pennies tossed off the pier,

I am from foot-long hot dogs, thick curly fries, and crisp knishes on night runs to Coney Island,

I am from sounds of Coney Island where music from the merry-go-round and cotton candy was loved by all,

I am from maple trees feeding the air with delicate scents of new buds each spring,

I am from the aromas of freshly baked bread and large crumb cake squares in local bakeries,

I am from building forts after snowstorms, sleighing in McKinley Park, snot sticking to my face and not caring,

I am from catching lightning bugs and housing them in jars with holes in the lid,

I am from playing stickball, hopscotch, kick the can, and skates with keys,

I am from Carvel's lemon ice and the Good Humor truck,

I am from trucks sauntering down the street offering services to sharpen knives, and the whip and Ferris wheel for excited kids,

I am from being sent out to play until dinner time,

I am from Campbell's tomato soup and grilled cheese sandwiches,

I am from answering the door for the doctor with his little black bag, men selling dictionaries, women selling Avon, and the Fuller Brush man,

I am from Sunday School every Sunday in patent leather shoes,

I am from laundromats and clothes lines, washboards, and washing dishes by hand,

I am from singing Rock of Ages with mom as I dried the dishes,

I am from hanging clothes on clotheslines even in frigid temperatures so dad's pants stood up all on their own,

I am from apartments with dumbwaiters that dropped garbage into cellar bins,

I am from prayers said out loud before laying my head on my pillow, and

I am from doing for others as I would want them to do for me.

When you put me in Sunday School, I wasn't tall enough to open the door to The Lutheran Church of the Good Shepherd. The hallways felt alien, their cold tiles making my tiny footsteps echo off the walls, a far cry from the colored blocks and games of kindergarten. I felt lost, not knowing what to make of the lessons the teachers wanted me to learn. I understood so little, wondering how God could love me without knowing me. You were so confident about God's love. I wanted to be confident too. It scared me to think of a man I didn't know having feelings about me. I wasn't sure what I was supposed to feel.

You insisted Sunday mornings were for God, and it was important to wear my patent leather shoes and lacy dresses, even though I protested. How come I could play stickball in the street on Saturdays in my dungarees but on Sunday I had to sit on the stoop with a doll, dressed up, all day, pretending it meant something to me? Sundays were sad. My male friends got to play stickball. I was envious of Peter, Douglas, and Robert as they ran up and down the street playing kick the can. I hated playing with dolls. I never quite knew what to do with them. I liked playing games in the street, running around, feeling alive.

I asked you how you knew Jesus loved me when he didn't even know me. You said it was true, but I still did not understand how you knew it was true. You were so sure. Did you believe he loved you too? Just in case you didn't, I doubted enough for both of us. Each night we prayed:

Now I lay me down to sleep
I pray the Lord my soul to keep
If I should die before I wake
I pray the Lord my soul to take.

You smiled, filled with pride for my acquiescence. I could not imagine what God knew about me to love me. I imagined faith was like Aladdin's magic carpet, a ride to another world.

NINE

It was winter and I stared into bare trees. My wool coat and hat did not protect me from the icy air as I fell into the chill, numbness spinning me into a motionless state, like being hypnotized. I dropped deep within myself, then heard my inner voice speak, "Will I have enough faith to endure my life?" Still as a tree, I stared down the street, facing my foggy breath. How does a nine-year-old make sense of such a thought? Shortly after, life felt different.

Karen James, my friend from school, moved away. She had given me The Grimms' Fairly Tales for my birthday, and I tried to enjoy the book, but the tales scared me and I couldn't understand why. Everyone said they loved them. I missed Karen. I liked having friends other than the kids on the block who were always fighting about something.

Then I made friends with Joyce Reid. She loved the piano, much to your delight, and when she came over she taught me to play a few tunes without having to read music or sit with a teacher with bad breath.

When Joyce died of complications from polio the spring of fourth grade, I was devastated. Thank you for letting me go with the class to say goodbye to her at the funeral home. We walked the six blocks in a single line; Mrs. Reinertson made sure no one deviated from her direction.

Joyce looked so pretty in that fairy tale blue dress she wore to one of her sisters' weddings. Her mother stood at the head of the casket with Mrs. Reinertson and told us we should be glad Joyce was now with God. I wasn't glad. I was mad. I was sad. I felt like crying but laughed out of nervousness and everyone looked at me and sneered. They didn't know Joyce was my best friend. They didn't know how much I was missing her already. Maybe that was when I started wondering about God and why he would take away my best friend. I knew I would miss her forever. And I was right.

I came home crying and ran to your room, burying my head in Grandma's afghan. You called out from the kitchen that Joyce was with God, and we should be happy. I couldn't believe you thought I should be happy when you knew she was my best friend. I didn't expect Mrs. Reinertson or her mother to know that, but you did. I told you how sad I was and would never play the piano again because it was too sad, and you kept saying Joyce was with God as if that should change how I felt. I was nine. God had no right to my friend!

I wanted you to come to your room and hold me and let me cry and talk about Joyce, but inside I knew how you felt about being touched. I remembered that day at the sink when I was five, and the time I wanted to nap with you when I was in first grade, but you didn't want me "on top of you" while you napped, so you handed me a book and pencil and instructed me to sit on the floor near you and circle all the instances of the word "to." What was it about you and touch, Mom? I could never understand that. I've seen my childhood photos. I was adorable. Didn't you have the urge to hug me—ever?

Joyce died right before school ended, so that had to be around May. Then in August Grandma died. I knew she had problems with her heart but losing her on top of Joyce was too much. It wasn't a stretch to see you didn't like sadness. You shared a dream you had the night before Grandma died. You told me you watched her climb a ladder into the golden sky and you awoke fearing it meant your mom had died. You and Dad and some relatives went to the hospital with flowers the next day only to come home with those flowers, your heads down, walking sadly to our apartment.

It was the dream you had that seemed significant to me, even as a nine-year-old. We often had the same dreams, prophetic, often disturbing dreams. You wouldn't let me talk about Grandma, nor would you, although sometimes you cried while Dad and I watched *Wagon Train* after you did the dishes. I was left drowning in sadness by myself. Your perfect shell was cracking, and I lost my footing. I wanted to cry all the time. I missed my best friend, and I missed going to the park with Grandma. Too much missing for my young life. I looked towards you but realized you were drowning too. All I could do to save us both was not to mention my sadness again. With the both of us drowning, we had no one to pull us up. Dad was even worse in handling grief having lost his dad when he was a young teen. Denying our grief was the closest we had to a life raft until the raft started sinking.

Like years in a tree's life, I started building circles around my heart, circles of protection, spirals of cracks and nicks secreting away accumulated losses. I started to become sensitive to the pain of others, my own simmering on the surface everywhere I went. I felt I was at the edge of such deep grief; I could have broken into a million pieces. I felt it as strongly as you feel hot water, but I had no idea what to do with it. My body began to turn against me, exhibiting migraines, headaches, stomach problems, dizzy spells, and anxiety. All this suffering erupting from hidden grief. As if that weren't bad enough, it got worse.

I was thirteen when we moved out of the apartment and

bought our first home with Grandma's inheritance. I loved that house. We couldn't enter it yet because the deal hadn't been finalized. You walked me to the back porch and asked me what I thought of it. I looked into the dining room window and saw what little I could through the blinds and in that moment, I gave that house my longing for attachment. But with it came an increase in expectation, because after we moved in you had your nervous breakdown over not dealing with Grandma's death. We all knew it. Even you, Mom. But you never mentioned it. Do you remember how we each coped? Well, here it is: Dad drank and got angry, my sister left the house for full days at a time, and I had the responsibilities for what you couldn't do as you laid on the couch gagging and having panic attacks. At the time I had no idea about panic attacks, I just knew your anxiety hit the roof.

I vaguely remember a time when you disclosed that you were grateful your mother left you enough money to buy a house but missed having her to share it with. For myself, I had hoped moving would give us a fresh start, a place without the past, a relief from all we never resolved. But I soon learned nothing in life stays behind, even when you move forward.

Even though I had the job of cleaning, ironing, learning how to bake or broil a chicken, making salads, doing laundry, and grocery shopping, I didn't mind helping you. I watched you on the couch trying to get up and do things. You weren't the type of mother to stop no matter how bad you were feeling, so when you couldn't get up, I knew you were too overwhelmed to think. When you could you did, but when you couldn't that was my cue, and despite feeling a great deal of pressure, it was a connection with you. You counted on me; I wanted to be there.

Then in high school, at sixteen, my friend Kathleen Wong got tuberculosis. We were all so happy when she got well enough to return to school, but one day she fell down the stairs and her bones broke into pieces. She never came back. I saw her at times in a wheelchair in her family's laundromat, and she had gained a lot of weight and couldn't walk. She soon passed away.

How much can a heart carry? Again, I grieved alone. I really don't know where I put it all. I thought not feeling it in the moment meant it went away. But that can't be true, because I can feel it now, Mom, as I speak to you about it all. You were so sweet to her parents after they lost their only child. I couldn't step into their laundromat. I just couldn't do it. I couldn't let myself break anymore. I know I let you down because you always did what was right no matter how you felt about it, but I just couldn't. You had such grit, and I loved that about you. I was always proud of you for it. You never backed down.

SEVENTEEN

After high school graduation I was grateful you took me under your wing, because traveling on subways and looking for a job was frightening. I was only seventeen. I depended on you for everything. You knew the working world well, having reentered it after we got into grammar school. You knew how to find a job and get around Manhattan. The working world was an alien world to me. You walked me into lobbies and told me how to ask if they had openings. I had no idea how to handle myself in this new world and it made me anxious that I might not be able to please a potential boss. I knew I had the excellent skills needed to be an effective secretary, but knowing things in high school and putting them to use in corporations were two different worlds.

Remember when I first entered the marble lobby at Western Electric and I approached the woman at the desk as you instructed? Remember how nervous I was? But it went so well. The woman told me they had openings, and I was quite excited. I couldn't wait to meet you at your office and tell you about it. With an interview lined up, I trailed behind you like a puppy to a busy restaurant for lunch. Your job was only a few blocks away on John Street, and if I got the job, we could travel together every day, maybe have lunch too.

I didn't tell you this because I felt naïve and stupid, and I suppose I was both, but going on the subways terrified me. I was so fearful of getting on the wrong train and being stuck underground not knowing how to find my way home. Another good reason to get a job close to yours, we could travel together, and I was relieved knowing I didn't have to learn the subway system too. I didn't tell you I thought working on Madison Avenue would have been more exciting, because I didn't like the thought of adventuring uptown alone.

The interviewer at Western Electric called and hired me, commenting that my secretarial skills were impressive. The tests revealed I took steno at one-hundred-ten words per minute and typed ninety words per minute. Remember my first salary mom? I made eighty-three dollars a week, eight dollars more than the average secretarial job because of my skills. They assigned me to Miss Buckley's secretarial pool at 83 Maiden Lane in their Department of Defense—just around the corner from you. I was surprised I got the first job I interviewed for. I was dreading having to do a lot of interviews.

My friend Diane Wilke didn't know how to get a job or manage the subways either, but her mother couldn't help her because she didn't work and she didn't go to Manhattan. Diane was grateful I could help her, but I couldn't have done it if you hadn't helped me. Ironically, and with glee, Diane and I not only got our first job at Western Electric, but our desks were next to each other in Miss Buckley's steno pool. How fortunate is that?

Up until then, it seemed you knew me better than I knew myself. You still held a little bit of magic for me, always knowing, always able. And although I didn't always like your decisions, I respected you, despite my opposition at times that made you think I didn't respect you. I was trying to earn respect for myself, my ideas, my creativity, my wanting to have my own direction. I was growing up. I don't think you liked that, and I think you enjoyed even less the fact that I no longer relied on you for money. I felt you were trying to hold me back from growing out of your control. I hated fighting for control when I simply wanted to learn how to live more on my own terms. I needed you to see that. But everything became a battle about whether I loved you or respected you.

The longer I made my own money the more you seemed to think I was threatening your authority. I was morphing, I was moving out of childhood, and I couldn't stay there just to make you feel better. Ironically, because of all the help you gave me, I was able to push out on my own. I wasn't as confident as you, but I was moving in that direction. The more confident I became, the less confident you became that I still wanted and needed you. It made me nuts.

Much of the time I continued to back down from my own life hoping for that ineffable moment when you would realize I was ready to have more independence and set me free. I sensed it was more than making my own money that threatened you. It was the essence of our relationship that was unraveling. The distance was beginning to increase, as if having my own identity as a daughter meant you were no longer viable as my mother.

I wish we could have talked about this, but your silent treatment kept me distant. My attempts to talk with you were met with irrational premises, and I felt I was in a spiritual warfare with you all the time. No one outdid you on the silent treatment, Mom, no one! How can you have a conversation with someone who has locked themselves away? Did you really want me to be so shut out from you while at the same time giving me hell for not coming to you? Ironically, the more you would have allowed me to slide away into my own life, the more I would have naturally gravitated towards you. Didn't you trust me, after all you taught me? Hadn't I proved how trustworthy I was after all I did to help you and after all you taught me?

Your deadly silent treatment was not silent. There was no

peaceful center. It felt like a death sentence, and to live in some peace I had to throw myself into the fire, a flame that would turn me to ashes. Fortunately, but also sadly, I was maturing enough to push back harder than I ever had, hoping to help you understand. I could not give up on myself just to please you, can you see that now, Mom? You used to yell at me that you were a dutiful daughter and why wasn't I? Did you not see I was trying to be dutiful to you? It wasn't easy balancing the duality of dependence and independence when the only part you accepted was my dependence.

When I got my dream job working for an attorney on Wall Street and made more money with exceptional benefits, you got angrier with me, even though I thought you were happy I got the job. Did I ever tell you *how* I got that job? I think I might have kept it to myself because there was a lot going on between us then.

One day, while still at Western Electric, I had lunch with a coworker. I told her I wanted to specialize my skills and work for an attorney, and she said her friend who worked for a large law firm on Wall Street was leaving to go to France with her boyfriend. She wanted to know if I wanted an interview, and I said "yes" before she finished her sentence.

The day of the interview was a miracle. I sat across from the attorney, not much older than me, and watched him pace in his small office thinking up questions for me. At one point, he stopped and asked me if I could take steno at 120 words per minute. When I responded, "Only if you can talk that fast," he asked, "Can you start Monday?"

I was surprised at my own boldness but knew I was somehow channeling you, because that was the kind of statement you would have made. Am I right?

He pressured me to start the next week, but I remembered what you taught me about always giving a company two weeks' notice to show respect. So that is what I insisted I had to do before I began working for him. He relented and I started the job after giving Western Electric their rightful two weeks' notice. I loved the people at Western Electric and it wasn't an easy leave, but I had a strong desire to advance to a more lucrative and exciting job. I wanted to follow my dream, because for the first time in my life, I had one.

The attorney and I got along, and I loved working for him. The firm treated their secretaries well and my life seemed to be going along just fine. Then a combination of things started happening. You were reactive to my happiness in a surprisingly hostile way; I fell in love for the first time, but he didn't love me; I was ready to live on my own with or without a man—meaning, I was ready to leave home. My friends were getting married one by one, but I wasn't, and I knew I had to do something.

Our arguments increased, and I could barely stand coming home from work every night. I couldn't understand why you were putting so much pressure on me about everything. It seemed I couldn't do anything right, but I was actually doing a lot right and I needed you to notice what I was going through was harder for me than you. I needed your help. I needed to share the reality of my disappointments and fears in where my life seemed to be heading and I needed your guidance. But you made yourself more inaccessible, and no matter what you blamed it on, nothing made sense. I seemed tethered to an unseen enemy.

It didn't matter what I did, what I thought, how I was feeling, what I did for you, what I didn't do for you—nothing made a difference, and our home was becoming a war zone rather than a safe place to rest. I started focusing on how to get away from you. I knew efforts to make you happy were sinking me into a dark abyss and if I didn't take care of my own happiness, I might never recover my life.

I liked to see people pleased and happy, but my existence

had become a light that flickered on and off with the approval of others, and it was driving me crazy.

I wrote you this poem, Mom.

KEYS

My mother gave me her dream
to play the piano to make me happy
to make her happy.

She enrolled me in
the best school with the best teacher
from the Julliard School of Music
where I was taught to
memorize classical pieces
and appear talented
to make me happy
to make her happy.

I played in recitals.
Fifty people clapped as I cringed.
I still knew nothing about the piano
But I did it to make her happy.
I was not happy.

I stopped the expensive lessons
seemingly ungrateful for
my mother's financial sacrifices
because I wasn't happy.
I meant to make her happy
she became more unhappy.

In high school I studied typing
hitting keys in speedy rhythm
creating a language I understood.
It made me happy
hoping it would make her happy.

I'm playing keys
that are black and white
just like the piano.
I am happy.

Are you happy yet mom?

TWENTY-TWO

After working as a legal secretary on Wall Street for three years, life changed yet again. It had been exciting entering historical office buildings with men in pinstriped suits, polished wingtip shoes, swinging leather attaché cases. It was glamorous, the smell of a new day, floors, desks, and chairs polished, smells of fresh coffee sitting on everyone's desks as I sat with my cup of tea and my steno pad, ready to take the next letter. I never thought of leaving all of it to sit in a classroom, take tests, do lengthy assignments for the next day. No one was more surprised than me when I decided to go to college at twenty-two.

But as you know, Mom, life is full of unexpected and unwanted surprises. New beginnings happen all the time. I never thought my new beginning would come about because of hardship. After all, things were going great, and I was making good money. I was on my way to success. I suspected any changes would be made through promotions and raises, accomplishments and celebratory moments. But here I was, watching all my friends go in one direction when my life was diverting into another. I felt successful at work but unsuccessful in my personal life.

Friends and co-workers began flashing diamond rings, making plans for all the changes married life would bring. I heard about their dreams, hopes, plans. They were buying homes and deciding on names for their future children. I, too, had fallen in love, but with a man whose temptations steered him towards other women. He said he didn't love me, and all I could do in that shocking moment was thank him for being honest. I was heartbroken and shattered. What else was I to do?

I did the worst thing a young woman can do—I thought if I could change him he would love me. I truly believed if he understood me, got to know me, he would fall in love with me. But the more I tried, the less difference it made. I did what all girls do, I tried harder. Then I did the next worse thing a young woman could do—I believed if he didn't love me, it said something about me. It said something was wrong with me. It meant I wasn't lovable, worthy, or enough. And of course, with that kind of thinking I became more distressed than ever. I never considered his not loving me was about him. I loved him, so he was perfect in my eyes. I never thought to ask myself if I loved me too. That's what I needed *you* for, Mom. I needed you to tell me I was lovable, and that any man who didn't love me wasn't worth my effort. I needed your support and comfort. Most of all, I needed you to show me the way out of such a toxic and painful relationship. But how could you do that when we were trapped in one ourselves?

I longed for you in a way only daughters could want their mothers at times like this. I longed to be soul soothed. I knew you and your first love broke up for the same reason. He got a nurse pregnant in WWII while overseas.

I understood why you didn't like my first love. I heard you on that one. He was more educated than my Brooklyn boyfriends. He had his own apartment in the Village. He was independent from his family. He lived outside the scope of Brooklyn, taking me to plays and restaurants you weren't familiar with. This was exciting to me. My world was expanding, and I wanted to share it with you, not threaten you with it. I wanted you to hear why

I loved him, how he was changing my life for the better, while at the same time breaking me. He broke me into smithereens, and I had no idea how to put myself back together. You had to notice how depressed I was. Had you ever seen me like that? I lost ten pounds, down from ninety-nine. Didn't you notice? Did Dad notice? My boss at work noticed. He told me how worried he was about me and wanted me to go talk to someone. I wanted that someone to be you, though he meant a psychiatrist.

For two years you watched me suffer, breaking up with him only to go back months later, and it was tearing my confidence. The power of unrequited love was unexplainable. Not realizing it because I was only twenty, I had put my worth into his hands. If he loved me, I was okay, and if he wanted another woman, I wasn't. I needed you to help me unravel the mess and instruct me to believe in myself. You were fearful I would stay with him, so you abandoned me. Your anger at me for my weakness in wanting him was intolerable. I needed your experience to help me extricate myself from him. Instead, I had to extricate myself from both of you. The only way I knew how to get free was to get out of New York, out on my own, but I needed help for that too. How could I do that without your help? You had been my roadmap. Now what?

I decided I'd go to college. I had no idea what I wanted to study but with no marriage in sight and a broken heart, college seemed a good alternative. If nothing else, I'd get smarter. When I told you I wanted to go to college you immediately started researching colleges within a train ride from Brooklyn so you could keep me at home. I panicked. That was the last thing I wanted. I was certain of one thing: we could not live in the same house together and maintain a civil relationship.

I was breaking all the family rules. Women in our family didn't leave home without a man. Well, Mom, times were changing. I was buying *Ms.* magazines and reading about

Women's Liberation. I saw marches all over Manhattan, women who threw their expensive bras into barrels of fire. I wonder, if Bay Ridge High School had allowed you to follow your dream to be a scientist back in the 1920s, would you have stepped out of the family rules too? Did the opportunities facing me remind you of all you had to give up?

I celebrated the new milestones with all my friends: engagement showers, bridal showers, weddings, buying homes, having babies. How could I not be happy for my friends? I went through the motions of daily life dissociating myself because I had no allies, just heartbreak and disappointment. There was too much pain deep inside myself to even think I had time or energy to conquer. The door had clamped shut. I was outside. I was suffocating in invisibility. So, I designed something new. Something I could engage in. A life that had hope. I began practicing yoga with Lilias Yoga and You every Saturday morning, reading books about Women's Liberation, joined The Book of the Month Club to read a variety of books, and worked my way through *The New York Times* crossword puzzle on the train going to work. The more I outgrew my childhood, the more depressed you got. We each needed the other to feel better, but that hope just made things worse.

I had no words for it back then. I don't know if I have words for it now, except to say the moat became wider the more time went on. We both felt it. If only we could have brought it out into the open and talked about it during dinner. As the years went by, it seemed to deepen into a chasm.

Then something unexpected and timely showed up.

One Sunday in early 1972, I spread *The New York Times* on my bedroom floor and prayed it would contain the answer for my future, because I had absolutely no idea how to change my life. You always had a litany of answers for everyday problems, but you wouldn't allow any conversation in which you didn't get your way. That wasn't going to work now. As a single woman, I was blue without a sky, a star without the moon. I started having my own panic attacks.

I couldn't tell you about my panic attacks. I didn't want to remind you of the panic attacks you had after losing Grandma. Now I was having panic attacks, and they were hell. I started avoiding people because my life did not resemble the expectations you set, and I was devoured in shame. I couldn't tell what was wrong with me, not just because I was in a panic most of the time, but because others gave me the impression I was doing something wrong since my first love didn't love me back. I was stunned at the insensitivity of people asking me about my failed relationship as if I were the failure. It got me riled up, heartbreak or not, because the assumption was getting married was the only calling for a woman. This was the 1970s, and women were marching down Madison Avenue and throwing their bras into fiery bins. Women's Lib, it was everywhere! I attached to it, not that I burned my bra, but I burned the dead dreams of who and what I was supposed to become.

I can't explain why I feel a strong desire to share these times with you now, Mom, but I do. I want to tell my story from my point of view and share how you were and still are impacting my life since you died. So, enjoy your grilled cheese sandwich, because I have a lot more to say.

The New York Times sprawled out on my bedroom floor. I made sure to read every page, every ad, every article. It took me three hours. I panicked when I got to the last page and hadn't found a single inkling as to how to change my stuck life. And then, I turned the last page over and thought I would burst from excitement. I stared at the full-page ad for the upcoming summer session at the nine state universities in California.

I ran to my typewriter, typed nine letters, then ran out the door to the corner mailbox and dropped them in. I wanted to run to you and share the good news, but it was only good news for me. For you, it meant a more emotionally hostile war.

I thanked God for my answered prayer. I told God no matter which university responded first, I would go. I didn't care which college selected me because I didn't know anything about any of them. I was willing to run to the edge of the wide horizon simply because there was one and it offered me a place to start again.

A few weeks later an acceptance letter came from the University of California/Santa Cruz. I waited until dinner to announce the news. Remember? I'm sure you do. My heart pounded hard in my chest, and I avoided your eyes. I looked at Dad, not that it was easier to tell him my news, but he wasn't angry with me. I knew this would hurt him because he, too, thought I should continue living at home until I was married and because Dad and I were very close.

I reticently made my announcement. Dad's face turned pale, his mouth stopped chewing, and he stared at you, his eyes begging for you to stop my madness. I looked to my left and you were seething. You lit a Pall Mall, gritted your teeth, and spewed such fire in your exhalation I thought my eyebrows would go aflame. I couldn't let your anger have power over me, not anymore. I was fed up with being fearful of you.

What was so wrong about wanting to go to college? If I only did what you approved, who would I have become? How would I know who I was? I needed to discover myself. I was crushed, a flower trying to grow in shallow soil after being repeatedly stomped on. This wasn't about love. I knew you loved me. This struggle between us, in my eyes, was your need to use me to fill the indefatigable emptiness from Grandma dying, along with your own buried dreams. It made me fearful to think about you dying because no daughter wants to entertain their mother dying no matter how much chaos resides between them. But it went deeper than that. I didn't want you to die before we worked out some form of healing. I didn't want you to leave me holding all the loose ends, the hostility, the things you misunderstood that I could have resolved if you took the time to listen and not condemn.

I was raw. I'm not saying this to hurt you or to strike out against you. I'm simply trying to find my honest and loving voice with you, as your daughter.

The day I left for college should have been a happy one. Instead, it was riddled with nerve-wracking breaths as the windshield wipers slapped hard against Dad's Impala. Each sound of the wiper jolted my nervous system. Not even a rainstorm could have washed away the toxicity of that day. I went to say goodbye to my sister, but she slid under the covers and wouldn't talk to me. She hated me. Did she know about your nervous breakdown? It didn't seem she ever stayed home long enough to pay attention to what was happening. All she knew was I was the one who had to tell her to behave—per your request because you were too sick to do it—when our neighbor complained about her stomping up the steps and screaming from the minute she got home to the minute she sequestered herself in her room after dinner. No wonder I had migraines and stomach distress.

Anyway, we headed to the airport, the road slick from water, the wipers slapping, Dad crying, and you not quite sedated enough from the Valium you had just swallowed. I sat in the back seat in sharp, stabbing silence, aching to have a moment of joy as I ascended into my new adult life, alone, a bird with no flight path.

I packed a few pairs of shorts, tops, and underwear thinking summer was warm everywhere. Dad had tied Great-grandma's quilt with heavy twine, and the only other possession I wanted to take with me was my Smith Corona typewriter I'd need for class papers. I never thought to check the weather to find out the temperature in Santa Cruz. I didn't know California got cold on summer nights; I didn't know I'd be in the mountains because Santa Cruz was on the coast.

You wanted me to explain why I bought a one-way ticket, but I couldn't muster up a way to tell you I wasn't planning on coming back after the eight-week summer session. Why would I set myself up for more distress? You made it so hard on me. I knew any conversation would result in more screaming and truthfully, Mom, I couldn't handle any more disapproval. I bought a one-way ticket because I didn't plan on returning to New York.

Finally arriving at the airport, Dad found the departure gate and parked. It would have been okay if you didn't want to wait with me until the plane left. I knew matters would remain tense. At the gate I watched you lean against the wall while Dad sat on a circular couch in the middle of the room. He sobbed so hard a stranger approached you and asked if your husband was having a heart attack. Do you remember that? I wanted you and Dad to put your arms around me, be excited for me, wish me the best, promise if I needed *anything* all I had to do was call. I held my disappointment close to my vest and felt I had to look out for you. You spoke to me in monosyllables. I went over to Dad and put one arm around him, trying to comfort him. I couldn't stop trembling. Dad wouldn't look at me. I knew he hated crying in public, but there was nothing I could do. I hurt everywhere. I suppose we all did. Again, I went up to talk to you, but you wouldn't talk to me.

I went to the counter to ask the flight attendant a question and jumped for joy when I saw my friend from Wall Street, Lorraine, coming off a TWA flight. She looked so beautiful in her new airline uniform. I hugged her tightly and told her I was glad to see her. I asked her to stay with me until my flight left because I feared I would collapse from all the tension between us. Excitedly, she said she couldn't wait to get home to her new husband, stepped aside, and ran out the door. I watched her exit the sliding door in disbelief. That was it. My only chance to get a kind word, and I didn't get one. My best friend left me standing in the middle of the lobby, in tears, begging for a few minutes of her time. But I understood her excitement. It lit up the entire lobby. And, truth be told, if I had been in her position I would have wanted to get home to my new husband too.

Finally, the call came to board my flight. I kissed you and Dad goodbye. I didn't know what to say or do to make my departure easier. I seemed to be failing everyone at a time when most families would celebrate the first member of their family going to college, especially the first woman. I truly wanted everyone to be happy. Why couldn't it have been a happy occasion? Once I took that first step down the ramp, I couldn't, wouldn't, look back. Sometimes we must break our own hearts to set ourselves free.

I found my seat and broke out in sobs, imagining you and Dad crying and blaming each other all the way home, asking yourselves what you did wrong and who was to blame. I wanted to relax and know that the two of you would help each other cope, but I knew better. I knew you would use my choices as fuel to attack each other. I dried my tears because people were beginning to avoid me while choosing a seat. I couldn't blame them, I didn't want to sit with me either. I was a crying mess. Then a man about Dad's age climbed over me and sat next to me by the window. We simply nodded to each other. I couldn't say a word. I was so close to screaming.

The pilot announced we were 3,500 feet in the air just as a flight attendant walked by. I asked her how I could get to Santa Cruz after we landed in San Francisco.

"You're on the wrong plane," she snapped. "You should be on a plane to San Jose."

I took a calming breath and braced myself. Fearful I would

unload my stress on her, I spoke with measured rhythm. "Well, the plane will be landing in San Francisco. My question is, how can I get to San Jose. Telling me I'm on the wrong plane while I'm 3,500 feet in the air doesn't help." I admit I snapped at the end of my sentence and felt no apologies. If I could have smacked her with dignity, I would have. But hitting people was not my style.

The attendant looked at me in disgust and quickly walked down the aisle. I couldn't stop trembling. She had given me the perfect opening to break out in sobs.

The man next to me leaned over. "I have a daughter your age. I'll help you once we get on the ground. You can take a Greyhound Bus to San Jose and then another to Santa Cruz."

I calmed enough to give him a faint smile and a weak "thank you." We talked about my plans, and he was gracious and sweet. He redeemed me for the rest of the flight. After the plane landed, he carried my typewriter to the Greyhound counter. I paid for my ticket and took a breath. I leaned on the counter and whispered, "I did it! I made it!" I was in California and on my own. The rest would be easy from here on out. But not so fast. Oh Mom, are you still listening?

During the Greyhound ride from San Francisco to San Jose, I noticed the majority of the ten passengers were college-aged. I asked if any of them were going to UCSC. It turns out eight of them were. Here is where I kicked into being a New Yorker, talking to strangers as if they were neighbors. I had watched you talk to strangers as if they were old friends, so now I did so too. I wished you could have seen me at that moment. I started a conversation and suggested we travel to UCSC together.

We arrived in San Jose a little after five and were told the last bus to Santa Cruz had just left. I had just gone through hell; nothing was going to stop me now. I surmised I was at least five years older than my new companions. They were quite freaked out about the situation. I calmed them and asked how much money they had. Taking charge helped calm me too, and as the oldest child in our family, I was used to emotional responsibilities falling on me.

I hailed a cab, but the sun was disappearing, and the cab driver did not want to go to Santa Cruz in the dark. I couldn't understand why he didn't want to drive in the dark. Isn't that when most people need cabs? I bargained with the thin, dark man, his marble-sized brown eyes studying me. I told him we would give him a good tip, but he pushed back. It seemed the road to Santa Cruz was quite mountainous, and he didn't want to drive Highway 17 in the dark. I had no idea what he was talking about, having never been on that road before, but I knew nothing was going to keep me from getting to the college, not the darkness nor a mountainous road.

"It will be dark soon," he kept saying.

"Then let's go!" I said.

He persisted. So did I. Finally, reluctantly, he agreed.

I knew how to handle this, Mom, only because I had seen you when you were determined to make something happen. You were the one who taught me strength when the odds were against you. Remember when Dad didn't want you to get a job, but you did it anyway? Remember when he didn't want you to spend several nights a week volunteering at the church, but you did it anyway? I studied you. I studied your strength, determination, and focus. Did you know that? The only time you gave up was when grief pulled you down to your ankles. You never got up from that one. I never saw you insecure until then.

There were too many unsaid moments between us, Mom. Too many. Pretending everything was okay when it wasn't only made life a lie, and it ate me up. How do you keep on keeping on when your life's huge moments live inside the hardness of a shell? I understood your pain. I lived it with you. The problem was now that I had my own pain to deal with, I was stuffing it down, just like you. In California I promised to change that part of my life. I wanted to give myself permission to speak the truth and only the truth. I wanted to crack the shell of deception that said everything was okay when it wasn't. I committed myself to changing the way I handled my internal life. I did not know how I was going to do that, but I made a vow going forward.

Forty-five minutes after we left San Jose, we arrived at the bottom of Highway 17, then drove up a short hill through a quaint neighborhood. The cab stopped in the most beautiful wooded area I think I had ever seen. The smell of redwood trees surrounding the university was pungently intoxicating; their pine needles blanketed the ground; their trunks were wide and deep, nestled among the buildings like a mother holding infants. I walked to a table to sign in.

"Where are you from?" the girl at the table asked.

"Brooklyn." I said, not looking away from the ocean's little golden sparkles feeding my needy soul. I was in the right place. I fell in love with my new life. The girl patiently waited for my attention. She nodded with a giggle, staring at my face.

Around me parents were wrapped in hugs, saying goodbye to their kids, tears welling their eyes, smiling at their children. My grief and longing thundered through my veins. I could barely contain myself. I brought Great-grandma's quilt closer to my heart and wondered if, in her wildest dreams, she would have ever imagined that someday the hard work she put into sewing her old clothes into tiny squares would one day comfort her great-granddaughter in the toughest and newest moment of her young adult life.

I ached to call you, Mom. But I just couldn't give up my moment of falling in love with life.

I thought back to my last vacation from Wall Street. It had been nine months ago that Lorraine and I had gone to San Francisco for our summer vacation. I remember standing on a cliff, staring into the black night with twinkling stars competing with the city's lights. The view filled my heart, and I knew I was going to come back here one day to live. I knew this was where I belonged, where I could see the sky and the wide horizon. I tied myself around that scene, undoubtedly knowing it would someday reel me back to it. For the nine months after our trip, I told people at work and friends that one day soon I'd go back to California to live. No one believed me, but I knew. I just knew I would return, and here I was, looking out at the horizon from the Santa Cruz Mountains. I was in awe. I was surprised by my own life. It was happiness, joy, love, grief, faith, hope, all wrapped up in one inhalation.

I was assigned a dorm room with an eighteen-year-old roommate. The first night was the worst. I spent the night restless, awake, and trembling. No matter what I did, I could not calm my nervous system. The next day my stomach was sore, and I could barely stand up. I went to the university health clinic and asked the doctor for a prescription for those little green pills Dr. Robinson had given me. Remember, Mom? Those little green pills I took since I was thirteen to calm me after your nervous breakdown? I asked the university doctor to get out his big red pill book and I could show him what they looked like. I would have called you for the name of the pills, but I figured I'd walk into an onslaught of questions and accusations I did not want to encounter. He told me he wasn't going to give me anything to relax.

"Take a yoga class," he quipped and ended our meeting.

Lucky for me I had been doing yoga on Saturday mornings. Remember how you used to watch me do asanas and think I was nuts? Well, now a doctor was telling me to take a class in yoga. And I did. They had them on campus, but I also knew how to do them by myself.

Mom, you would have loved my classes. I wished I could

have shared them with you without you getting hostile. So, I'll tell you now.

The first class I took was in anthropology and I fell in love with the study of digging for old artifacts. I wanted to major in that. Then I took a sociology class and fell in love with that. Everything was new and exciting. I became thirsty for all I didn't know. I couldn't study enough, and l watched myself open and make space inside me for all possibilities. Remember when I was a kid and you looked up at the sky and wrote a poem? That's how I felt, Mom. I looked up and the magic was all there. I could do anything. But once again, the shadow of your sadness appeared, and I thought of your unrequited love for science. I thought of your dream of being a scientist crushed by Bay Ridge High because girls were secretaries and did not have jobs in science. How maddening! Guilt seeped its way into my peace, and I couldn't shake it at first. It kept finding its way onto my shoulders. I suffocated myself on all I couldn't tell you, but the redwood trees and the ocean did a good job of soothing me with their sounds, scents, and presence. The natural environment was my refuge.

The next class I took was Philosophy 101 and fell in love. That was it. I was going to study philosophy. I couldn't believe I was taking a class that focused on thinking, and I couldn't get enough. *Imagine, a class on thinking!* That was just what I needed. To be able to study the mind, my mind. It was both daunting and luxurious. I was raised to think a certain way because it was dubbed the right way, but now I had a professor walking up and down the aisles telling me all the possibilities of how to think and presenting philosophers who demonstrated those ways.

His name was Professor Carlos Norena, a robust Spanish man with enthusiasm so wide and deep I felt as if I fell into him every time he spoke. I'd never met a teacher like him before. His enthusiasm and passion were contagious. There was no way to listen to him and not be moved to enter the deepest part of yourself. He encouraged me to open my world, gave me permission to think for myself, and let me drop into my own curiosity without guilt, shame, or the need to be right or wrong, but to question everything and decide for myself. His class was a cool shower on a hot day. I couldn't get enough.

The best part, Mom, he fed me hope. You would have loved him. He reminded me of you before Grandma died. He didn't provide the kind of hope that said I could be smart someday, but the kind of hope that said I was smart right now. I felt I was breathing for the first time in my life. I felt alive and whole even though I was still experiencing tough times with you. Imagine feeling whole even though you aren't sure who you are yet. Oh, I wanted to rush to the phone and call you. What daughter wouldn't want to share this moment with her mother?

One day a boy in class complained that he didn't understand the philosopher we were studying and he felt stupid. Professor Norena walked up and down the aisle holding open a book and calling out to all of us, "If any man can write these words, any one of you can understand them. Each of you has the capability to understand what this philosopher is saying." I remember it so clearly because in that moment I found another piece of myself.

That moment imbedded itself into my soul. I swallowed it whole. I tucked it into every cell. It seeded a belief in my own potential, my own world of possibility, and an endless space for me to enter. No longer was I the kid who had to go to remedial reading or who had the near lowest grades in sixth grade. Slowly it dawned on me that I never really stood a chance to be present mentally in school. I had so much emotional responsibility at home. Don't get me wrong, I didn't mind helping or obeying. I minded being given the emotional weight you and Dad should have taken care of. I was the oldest, but the responsibilities I was given still exceeded my maturity level. Okay, I'll move on now.

I matriculated in philosophy. No matter what philosopher I studied I bought as many books by them as I could afford, not because they were required, but because I couldn't drink in enough new ways of exploring my own mind. My mind lost its borders, my prejudices, my limitations. My mind opened, a free energy, thirsty and searching for more awareness. That awakening was empowering. The best part was I was developing my own beliefs and expectations for my life. Life was no longer about fitting in, belonging to one set of thoughts or behaviors. Instead, I saw the world as limitless, with choices that would assist me in creating the beautiful, successful, loving woman I dreamed of becoming. It was an amazing experience, but also confusing and daunting. I was still trying to find my balance and to feel as if I were home inside myself.

I met a student named Tamara in one of my classes. We became friends and often sat on top of one of the mountains overlooking Monterey Bay. We liked sharing our different lifestyles, families, and interests. Her parents were in the camps in Germany during WWII. They had just married when they were separated and sent to the camps. Tamara and her family had experiences I had never heard of before. She introduced me to the diaries of Anais Nin whose writings continued to open my world and whose experiences introduced me to a life of choices I had not heard of before. I read all her diaries twice. Anais Nin stirred my desire to write, and I wanted to write like her—abandonedly, honestly, fearlessly.

When I worked on Wall Street, I wrote the words of others on a steno pad, then typed those words. However, I never got to know what my own words were. Does that make sense? Now, I yearned to write, to set myself free with inner language, to find out what words I wanted to use to understand my own emotions, thoughts, experiences, and relationships. Writing seemed like a great way to learn about the self and study one's mind. I wanted to give it all to the pen and let it speak for me. Between writing and philosophy, I was overflowing with excitement. I didn't have to think about what anyone needed and forget myself. I could focus on me, and it made me feel guilty, a little shameful, but overall excited.

Remember when you bought me the Girl Scout Diary, the one with the little gold key? I had just begun to write daily when that diary came up missing. I never found it again. Why you had a habit of taking my things and giving them away, I never understood. What could my ten-year-old self have written that was so bad that you had to take it from me? After that I stopped writing. Want to know why I stopped reading too, Mom? Remember all the books I had—Clara Barton, Hardy Boys, Nancy Drew? I loved those books, and I was still reading through them when one day I came home from school and they were gone. I asked you where they went, and you said it was time I let kids whose parents couldn't afford books have mine. I was angry with you.

Why would you buy me things and then give them away? Were you trying to teach me something or get praise from the church for your donations? What I learned from that wasn't how to be generous, because I am generous. What I learned was I couldn't trust you with my things, especially those I enjoyed. Why wouldn't you want to care about the things I cared about instead of giving them away? I've heard stories from other women whose mothers used to give away their things too. I don't know if I will ever understand that one.

Anyway, one sunny afternoon while sitting on the hill staring into the tops of the Redwoods, I casually mentioned to Tamara that I missed my friends and family back on the East Coast.

"Why don't you take up writing and become your own best friend?" she asked.

That did it. What Anais Nin stirred in me, Tamara broke

open.

I got up and ran to the bookstore, bought a composition book, and ran back to show her how she ignited a long-time desire, and I was so grateful for her encouragement.

In the beginning, I wrote about how anxious I felt about entering a new life without any interest from my family. Not one of you ever asked about my California life. It truly hurt. Anyway, I wrote out my frustrations about you. I wrote and wrote about everything. I wanted to know who I was. What was I meant to do? Was there a reason why the people I loved so deeply seemed so antagonistic towards me simply for wanting to live my dreams? I couldn't understand anything in my life. So, I wrote about it all, trying to understand what was happening to me and how I wanted my life to feel. I became a top spinning out of control, falling off the table, with no gravity to head me towards any direction. And each time I felt like that I picked up my pen and wrote until I couldn't write anymore. I didn't go back and read what I wrote. The writing was enough.

In one of my classes I was given the task of making a collage. The TA handed the class dozens of magazines and a poster board. She wanted us to draw a line down the center of it. On the left we were to paste pictures that resembled our past, and on the right we were to paste pictures of our present and future selves. We sat on the floor cutting and pasting, and when I was finished, I stared at my board. On the left side were pictures of a girl being oppressed. I had pasted a picture of an upside-down glass bowl with a girl inside it. On the right side were pictures of girls dancing in wide open fields, bouquets of flowers around happy people. I suppose that said it all. I knew where I was headed even though I wasn't sure what steps to take to get there.

The summer session was nearing its end, and I kept praying to God to give me a way to stay in California. I wanted to be that girl dancing in a field of flowers that I'd pasted on my poster board.

I talked to a few therapists at the college but none of them knew how to explain my emotions or had insights on how to deal with your anger. I kept writing and hoping that I would figure it out myself. Writing became my anchor. Wherever I went, I took my journal. I wrote in coffee shops, before bed, staring into the tops of redwood trees, and when I awoke in the morning. And I wrote about you a lot. I wrote about the love I had for you and how distressing it was that you would not believe I loved you. I wrote about my dreams and plans. I couldn't and wouldn't give up on myself just because I felt abandoned by you.

Sometimes I could feel God's presence as I wrote, as if a warm shawl had been cast over my shoulders. I felt God's grace, Mom, or maybe it was an angel, I don't know. I knew a Spirit was sitting with me. It is difficult to explain, but at the time the moment felt visceral, almost tangible. It was a certainty, a knowing that everything was unfolding before me as it should. But would you have listened if I said that to you? It seemed my gains became your losses. When I wrote, I entered a deep silence that allowed me to be truthful with myself. It was a sense of peace.

Within those emotional crevices I settled into a feeling like the one I felt in church after everyone finished a group prayer and the church got quiet. In writing from this space, all seemed right with the world, because in that moment of writing I felt whole even in my agony and fragmentation. All the tension, the misunderstandings, the pain of love melted into my words and fell visibly onto the page. The more philosophy I read, the more philosophical language I tried to apply to my own life. Without journal writing, I don't know how I would have synthesized the chaos of my emotional self.

As I was praying for a way to stay in California, I got a phone call. I hadn't planned this, Mom, and I know you thought I had. My first love was on the phone wanting to tell me his news, and as disturbing as it was on many levels, it was an answer to my prayer. I really left New York to get away from memories of him. You were part of it, but not the main reason. It was the only way I knew to give my broken heart a chance to heal. Get away—just get away! California was just far enough.

He told me he had been accepted to Stanford Law School; he was so excited. I was horrified. He never mentioned applying to law school when we were dating. I knew I still wasn't strong enough to be around him. What could I do? I wanted to stay in California, and I was going to need help. Given all you and I had been going through, Mom, I couldn't return for fear we would sever our relationship with all the hostility, and we might not ever return to each other. I couldn't call you about this one, so I called my friends from Wall Street, Nancy and Barbara. I wanted to share with them what I couldn't share with you. I mentioned I wanted to stay in California. I wasn't going to allow his arrival to persuade me one way or the other. I wanted to stay in Santa Cruz and reminded myself that California is a big state.

They shook my world with news that two of the attorneys from the New York firm had just started their own law firm in Palo Alto. Nancy said I should check it out. I had no idea where Palo Alto was. I hung up and asked my roommate where Palo Alto was. She said it was only forty minutes away on Highway 17, that infamous highway I talked the cab driver into driving over the day I landed in California eight weeks ago. She said Palo Alto was where Stanford was. *Stanford*? Did I hear her right?

Oh Mom, my first thought was that you would never believe I didn't pre-plan this synchronicity. I agree, the turn of events certainly looked suspicious. I would have been full of doubt if someone had told me this too. And yet, another prayer was answered when I called the law firm in Palo Alto and spoke to one of the attorneys. He remembered me from when I worked for George Grumbach on the twenty-sixth floor and when I once helped him when his secretary was on vacation. I explained I was in Santa Cruz and wanted to stay. I asked him if he was going to need a secretary.

"I just fired my girl last week," he said. "Can you start next Monday?"

"Yes." Yikes!

I became frantically excited. Now I had to get you to send the money in my savings so I could rent a place of my own. You hesitated. You were livid.

Reluctantly, I called my first love. I had more than mixed feelings about it. I couldn't believe he would be living in the dorms at Stanford, just a few blocks from the law firm where I just got a job.

I asked if he would help. He said he would and agreed to let me stay in his dorm room because Stanford did not have any other place for guests. I told you my plan, hoping you would feel relieved knowing I wasn't alone and that I had help. Naïve, yes, but honest just the same. The longer you took to send my money, the longer I had to stay with him. If only you believed me that staying with him was temporary until you sent my money. Instead, you told me I had planned this beforehand; you didn't believe things were fortuitously falling into place. I just wanted you to know I was with someone you knew and that I was safe.

You told me *I* would have to tell Dad I was staying in California and used my closeness with him to guilt me with your usual comment that I would kill him over this. I braced myself. I loved and adored Dad and I missed him so much.

But when dad got on the phone and I told him I was going to stay in California and already had a job with lawyers from New York, he simply said, "I miss you. I don't agree with your decision, but I'm here if you need anything." Then he hung up.

I cried knowing he was devastated. I could hear it in his voice. I also knew the scene that was probably taking place at home. You and Dad yelling at each other, blaming each other; I imagined you sitting at the table smoking one Pall Mall after another, wringing your hands and biting your nails. I had seen it a hundred times and it broke my heart. I wanted the two of you to make plans to visit me, to care about my life in California, to ask questions. It seemed unfair to feel happy while causing insurmountable distress for you and Dad. My ex didn't love me, but you both knew he would never deliberately put me in harm's way. Didn't that mean anything?

My roommate and her boyfriend were able to drive me to Palo Alto to meet up with my first love. Only God could have arranged so many details in such perfect order.

After you finally sent a check from my account, I rented my own apartment and purchased a used VW Bug. I'd always wanted a VW Bug, although my Rambler Ambassador at home had a lot more pick up.

As you once impressed upon me, it was important to have marketable skills. Having excellent secretarial skills kept me from having to take out large school loans. I enrolled in Foothill Junior College, which was only a short distance from my job, to earn my general education credits. After I saved some money and finished some classes, I planned to re-apply to UCSC to finish my degree in philosophy.

I hated working for the attorney in Palo Alto. He was a pig. He used to call me into his office to take a letter while hiding behind the door. As I entered his office, he would close the door behind me, throw me on his desk, assault me, and try to get me to kiss him. It was quite a struggle to get free of him, but I did. I never screamed. I never told anyone. I needed the job too badly. It was 1972 and I was only twenty-two. One week before my two-week vacation, the attorney belittled me in front of a client. That was the last straw. Something snapped inside me; I turned and walked out and never went back. He sent my friend Marilyn, another secretary for the firm, to my home to get me to come back. He didn't even have the courage to show up himself. I told her to tell him he was a coward and could get someone else to take his crap. He could keep my vacation money. I needed the money, but I'd rather find another way to earn it than sacrifice my integrity.

I looked for other jobs and quickly got them because of my marketable skills. I still saw my first love at times, but I knew how fragile I still was around him. I still loved him, and it was like swallowing glass every time I saw him. It's difficult to explain why I was still attracted to him. Getting him out of my system was like trying to get gum off my shoe. He still wanted to see me, but he still wanted to see other women too. I did not own him, nor did I ever expect to. Eventually, we moved further apart until I finally had to end it. I felt as if I had lost a part of myself and vowed never to let any man ever take a part of me again. I wanted something within me to keep forever, to stabilize me through losses and emotional hurts. I got busy coming up with interests and passions no one could ever take away.

It was a long haul, working and taking out loans, sharing houses and apartments, anything to keep my life moving in the direction of finishing school. I found it taxing but empowering to manage my own life. As soon as I got the needed credits from Foothill Junior College, I planned on leaving Palo Alto to matriculate back to UCSC. One of the guys I met at Foothill College called me. He had graduated the semester before me and was living in the dorms at UCSC. He wanted to know where I was going after Foothill, and I told him I was heading back to UCSC. He said he couldn't deal with the dorms anymore and wanted to know if I wanted to rent a place with him. I practically jumped through the phone with excitement. That one summer in the dorms was a nightmare, and I had no desire to return to them. I welcomed sharing a place with someone I already knew and trusted.

To say I sacrificed comfort during those college years is an understatement. A few friends visited from New York and couldn't believe I was living with old broken items from yard sales. A few told me they wished they could leave New York and strike out on their own, too, but weren't willing to make sacrifices. They'd tell me about their Ethan Allen furniture, how wonderful it was to be married, flash fingers with large diamond rings. Yet, I could sense their dissatisfaction, and I brought it up to them. Each one declared they couldn't stand the shame of being single "at our age." I started getting announcements for the birth of their first children. They seemed to have it all, but even through their announcements, letters, and phone calls, I could sense they would have preferred to strike out on their own than do what everyone else was doing.

I began making my own clothing because I couldn't afford to shop at department stores except for absolute necessities. At first, I cut out patterns and sewed by hand, then I had a roommate with a sewing machine, and she helped me sew by machine. I had nothing in the way of possessions to speak of. I ate hot dogs, packets of Lipton soup with hot water, and large pots of stuffed cabbage.

Disciplining myself was tough, but I kept looking forward and refused to regret anything. I could survive saying "no" to luxuries because I was on a path with a purpose and a mission. I loved being creative, pulling together something from nothing. And I appreciated it when you sent me a hundred dollars for a mattress, so I didn't have to sleep in a borrowed sleeping bag on the floor. It meant a lot that you were willing to help me with that, Mom. I'm sure you were biting your nails even further to the cuticle, because resisting me was a strong way to let me know you disapproved of my moving 3,000 miles away from home to go to college. But I was glad you helped when I needed it. It was tough getting good sleep on the floor despite the shag carpeting.

Remember my visits home, Mom? I started going home for three weeks during semester breaks, but you did not make it easy on me. When you greeted me crocheting baby clothes and telling me you were waiting, just waiting, it was devastating. Did you not see the look of pain on my face? In college I was getting educated, learning about myself, giving myself an opportunity for a better future. You never asked about my life. It tore through me.

I overheard you tell our neighbor I was studying journalism. I cringed. If only you let me explain. I remember walking by the two of you sitting on the brick stoop. "Philosophy," I quipped. "I'm studying philosophy, Mom." You didn't say a word.

Funny how memories stick with you. Whenever I sewed a piece of clothing, I thought of you. I remember when Dad bought you a sewing machine and you started making us matching skirts. You made me a large bag for my toys. Remember the dolls you made from little circles of colored fabric, each circle pulled with a string around its edges, all strung together to make the body and long floppy legs of a doll? How I loved those dolls. I wished I had one. I never liked playing with dolls, but I loved those fabric dolls. Did I ever tell you that?

I suppose I was five when you made the two of us matching skirts. We walked down Fifth Avenue and sang "I've Been Working on the Railroad." People looked at us as we sang, and we walked tall and proud. It was fun, and I remember being in awe of how pleased you looked. I remember thinking this was how I could make you happy. But then I grew up.

I think our crises crashed together: you, a mom going through menopause and watching her daughter go into the world without her, and me, a daughter making her own decisions and finding meaning and purpose for her own existence, while feeling abandoned and needing motherly comfort.

After returning to UCSC, my first love and I continued to see each other. I found myself emotionally right back where I left off in New York. My suffering overwhelming again. I wanted to end it but couldn't. My love for him had such a tight hold on me. And then I had a dream. You'll love this, Mom. We should have written a book about our dreams and how they came true. We could have made millions.

I dreamt I was walking on a tightrope between two tall apartment buildings similar to the one he lived in. Some of the tightropes had clothing on them, but the one I was trying to balance on didn't; not sure what that meant. Anyway, I was equidistant between the two buildings when my fear of heights kicked in. Then I heard a voice tell me to step down. *How can I step down?* I thought. *I'm high in the air.* I couldn't even look down. The voice insisted that I step down. I panicked. It was such a crazy thing to do on a tightrope. I finally looked down and saw I was about two feet from the ground, so I stepped down into the alley and the dream ended. This dream quelled my fear of ending the relationship. The next day I called him and broke it off. That time the breakup was permanent. I never saw or heard from him again.

FOR GIRLS ONLY

in the bedroom hallway
waiting like a ghost –
unadorned
cedar-wood hope chest –
corpse-like
not for my death
but for my life's
new beginning –
it wasn't

a gift
of love
it was to be earned
through obedience –

when I married
sacrificing my voice.

Only then those
handmade items
would be mine
only by the sacrifice
of my soul
conjoined to a husband's
could I earn the
familial belonging.

Unmarried I deserved nothing
no celebration into adulthood
no showers
no gifts
no honoring
unworthy
as my own woman.

Girls
Hear me now
no one can steal your hope –
it doesn't work that way,

that's all.

When I first moved to Santa Cruz, you asked me what Santa Cruz had that Brooklyn didn't. I wasn't sure how you wanted me to answer, Mom, because I knew no matter how I answered it, you would have been angry. You usually seemed to have only one answer that would soothe you. It was tough trying to second guess you.

So now I want to answer that question. Moving out on my own was stepping through a heavy curtain into the sunlight. I was twenty-two and ready to find out what the world had to offer besides heartache. In both Santa Cruz and Palo Alto there were large lots assigned to wild horses. Imagine driving home and seeing enormous, magnificent horses running wild through the meadows and trees. I felt as if I were breathing for the first time in my life.

I loved setting up an apartment, a meager home due to a lack of possessions. My first apartment in Palo Alto was furnished, so I didn't need much, and later all I really needed was a mattress and a table for writing. I lived simply to simply live. I had little, I needed little. I moved a lot, but I didn't mind. I simply loved it all. California was beautiful whether I lived near the mountains or the ocean or both. Was it all easy? Hell no. I had to manage my loans on meager salaries while paying school expenses and ordinary living expenses.

It seemed everywhere I went students were debating for their rights. Women wanted to be in charge of their healthcare, earn better incomes, be single if they wanted. It was a time when women were creating a world of their own design. The frustrating part for me was we had to do it by asking permission from men. So absurd. Why would men be in charge of us anyway? I had one class on women's lib issues, and in it there was one male. The teacher asked him why he was there as this was a class for women. I loved what he said: "Because I want to understand what women want and I can't do that in other classes." How fabulous his pursuit. I talked with him after the class, and he was so confused and interested in why women were protesting. He never realized women must earn rights whereas men didn't. To me you earn salaries, you don't earn rights. A right is a given. Only privileges are earned. I was still trying to extricate myself from your control, let alone men too. Perhaps that was more my problem.

It was an empowering time to realize how disempowered I was, and I know you ached for such a time as that to live. I watched you protest your right to work when Dad said he made enough and he wanted you home. I watched you design your life to get back into the working world once your kids were in school. I watched you step out at night to volunteer for our senator in Brooklyn, create events to earn money for the church, become a Brownie and Girl Scout leader. I watched you do this all with Dad's frustration. He wanted you home with him, that's where you were "supposed" to be. But you lived your life on your terms as much as you could without causing a divorce.

I attempted to explain it, Mom. Yes, Santa Cruz was beautiful, beaches and nature everywhere, but what it really offered was the opportunity for me to find out who I was, be in a new environment, meet new people, learn new things. That's what it had, amazing possibilities for me.

Anyway, one of my roommates, Chris, brought home a German shepherd puppy. At first, I was furious. How could we afford a puppy? We barely had enough money with our loans, which I got as a woman in a women's reentry program and he got as a Vietnam vet, to care for ourselves. The dog was home alone a lot since we left early in the morning and arrived home after three. Often the dog destroyed something. One time I came home to find he had pulled all the director chairs Chris and his dad had made into the center of the room. All the large pillows I made to sit on were torn and stuffing was everywhere.

He had pulled down our phone and destroyed the entire thing, and he had jumped on the counter and ate the pork chops I was defrosting, leaving only bits and pieces of aluminum foil on the floor. Then I went up to the bedroom and my Vanity Fair underpants were chewed up and laying on my mattress. The house looked as if a tornado had come through it.

Eventually I learned to love Nietzsche. He was a really good dog, and as he spent time with me, he became quite protective. One hot day I took him and ventured onto beaches few people knew about. I soon noticed I could go anywhere anytime I wanted with no fear of anything happening to me. Nietzsche would have defended me against anyone out to harm me. He looked ferocious, like one of those police dogs no one wants to pet, but he was a sweetie. I took him for a walk one night along the coast. Not one person out for a walk approached me and I realized an inner safety and freedom I never felt before. I remember asking myself if this was how men felt all the time.

Meanwhile, my hungry self ate every life experience I could get. I roamed the beaches, got in my car and drove up to San Francisco and down to Monterey and Carmel, found little tea houses to write in, discovered wooded areas for hiking. I found being alone wasn't the horrible experience you always told me it was. I liked being alone, not all the time, of course. I made a lot of friends and had people to do things with, but being alone got me to befriend myself. I loved the silence, the simple beingness of sitting under a fragrant redwood tree and eating an orange. It made the orange taste better, if you can believe that.

I got to feel who I was, what I was feeling, good or bad, and had time to consider what I wanted without the requests of others. I fell in love with my life. My emotional sensitivity no longer bothered me. I began to rely on it for the truth about what I was feeling. I wrote and wrote and then wrote some more. It seemed I was slowly awakening, although back then I had no words to fully describe it because I was tucked deep inside the blooming process. It was a time of naivete, innocence, and cracking open to awareness all at the same time.

I went to the ocean often and loved watching the full moon in the middle of the night ripple on the black ocean waters. I could watch those white ripples for hours and enter a deep dream state, letting them take me to an internal peace I never knew existed. I'd forget the struggles with uninteresting part-time jobs and loans and a desk full of assignments to complete on subjects I struggled to understand. Those nights by the ocean made an internal sense of home.

I started making wonderful friends like John. You remember John, Mom. We were roommates in Palo Alto. He stayed with us for a few days on winter break then ventured off to Baltimore to spend Christmas with his family. We are still friends today. I remember how much you liked him. And Bill, one of our other roommates who saw me struggling with my first logic class and told me once I began to understand the concepts I wouldn't struggle with it anymore. He sat with me until the equations made sense. Then I began to love deciphering the logic of arguments. After that, I got an A or A-plus on every exam and paper. I started feeling capable in taking on new challenges.

I had mostly wonderful roommates. I learned a lot and I enjoyed having intellectual conversations often sitting at the dinner table for hours. If I had unlimited money, I would be a perpetual student. Like you, Mom, I love learning. See? We were never far from each other.

And then the day came. After all the working at menial jobs, late hours studying until Johnny Carson, doing without, eating soups and stews, learning to grow veggies and make my own clothes, the day had come. I watched my roommates; their celebration seemed so simple. No grief. Just celebration. I struggled not to envy them. I had my own life to face and manage; I couldn't let myself get jealous. It wasn't easy but I was always good at self-discipline, so I succeeded in keeping celebration first, grief second.

Okay, now I'm going to get back to my story.

TWENTY-SIX

I sent you an invitation to my graduation but heard nothing back. I suppose I was being naïve, again.

I remember when we lived in the apartment. I was a kid when our neighbor Andrew used to spend all night in the cellar studying while his wife and kids slept. You incessantly praised his devotion to working hard to make a better life. I secretly hoped you had the same pride in me for all I sacrificed. I wanted you to share those praises with me because I was working hard and sacrificing for a successful life too.

I sent you that invitation to my graduation, wishing you would surprise me and be at the ceremony. I refused to let myself believe my own mother would ignore me after all the years I studied and worked to pay for my education.

I hoped I would discover you and Dad sitting in the front row like I did when I was five and danced at Carnegie Hall in Miss Lorraine's dance class. I remember seeing you and Dad smiling, and I knew that even though I was scared on stage—most of us were lost and looking around for what we should be doing—you and Dad were happy for me. Grandma was there too. I remember watching her walk backstage after the performance, which didn't go all that well, with an arm full of long-stemmed red roses for her ballerina star.

I remember it all, Mom. Even how you kept filling my patent

leather tap shoes with baby powder to ease my blistered feet so I could tap to "I'll Be Down to Get You in a Taxi, Honey." Oh, those blisters were awful! Poor Miss Lorraine. She was beside herself watching us trip over each other after all our rehearsals that never quite sunk in. I understood, even at five, your inspiration to get me to dance at a young age. I can remember so clearly your instructions in our apartment living room as you taught me the Lindy, Fox Trot, and Cha Cha with such joy that you lit up the room. I must admit it was fun. You were so happy when Dad was willing to learn the Fox Trot so you could take him out dancing. When you danced, it was like watching a prayer in motion.

* * *

My graduation wasn't a cap-and-gown ceremony. I found an affordable long dress that, except for the darts needing to be taken in a little, was quite pretty. Cousin Joannie came to the event, and it was great to have her there.

I met my friends' families who flew in from all over the country for graduation. There was a lot of happiness that day. The sun was warm, and spring had begun. Everyone was in a celebratory mood. The dense redwood forest was alight with rays of sunshine, and I felt as if I were walking through fields of yellow silk ribbons to get to the right building. Honestly, mom, I couldn't shake the longing, and a deep sharp pain of feeling abandoned by you. I wanted to share my accomplishment with you the way my friends were with their families. But you really didn't know how hard I worked or how much I sacrificed because you didn't want to hear it. A black curtain had been drawn between us, and no matter how hard I tried, I couldn't lift it. Grief had become my companion but, on this day, I didn't want it. On this day, I wanted the celebration I had earned. *Earned!* To lift my spirits, I imagined you sitting at the kitchen table secretly happy for me and wishing you had come.

The buzz in the air was constant; lots of hugs, winks, kisses all around me. The atmosphere was alive and joyful.

The audience settled, the happy buzzing about stilled, and the stage lit up as the students were cued to walk on stage. One of the professors began to announce student names. I watched each classmate walk across the stage to get a diploma as the next in line waited to hear their name. With each name, the audience roared with delight, clapping and hollering their cheers. Then the audience silently waited for the next name to be called.

I heard my name. My heart raced, my breath stuck in my throat, I think I left my body for a moment. I was lost in the power of the moment. *Finally!* I focused on the professor at the other end of the stage holding my diploma tied with a blue ribbon. All those years of work and sacrifice now came down to this moment.

I took a deep breath and stepped onto the first step, then the second step, then the third step, until I was finally on the platform. I heard my rubber-soled sandals hit the floor. Slowly I paced my steps towards the professor. As much as I wanted to hold my diploma, I also wanted to savor the moment. The professor seemed so far away. Here it was, Mom, the moment. I could hardly contain myself.

The auditorium sat shrouded in thick silence as I awaited applause. Each step I took sounded louder, the air still ensconced in silence. I heard my breath thump hard in my chest. I choked on the silence. It was deafening. Why was everyone quiet? I heard my heart scream in anger. *This is not going to happen. I am not invisible. I earned this moment.*

A forceful and huge push rose up inside me. I almost didn't recognize myself. I stopped walking; I wasn't going to leave the stage without *something* from the audience. I turned and faced them, looked parents in their eyes, and broke out in a wide smile, pretending you and Dad were seated in the front row. Unexpectedly, but with the strength of a train, I raised both arms and frantically waved to your imagined presence. I saved myself in that moment from despair. The imagination is powerful. Seeing you there, even in my private fantasy, raised my spirits. I widened my smile.

Then, I heard a lonely clap break the frozen air in the far back of the room to my right. Then I heard another meager clap. Then, dead silence. But I got my moment! That's what I really earned that day—I earned myself back. When dozens of parents made me feel invisible, I claimed my right to be visible. Such a silly way to put it. I guess another way to say it is in that moment I had compassion, honor, respect and love for myself. I gave myself permission to receive the love I wanted. Those two people who clapped for me might have done so out of pity, watching me walk onto the stage drowning in silence, but I emerged just the same. I refused to be invisible. Can anyone give themselves a better gift?

I turned back to walk across the quiet stage to the professor patiently waiting, my degree in his hand. I had almost forgotten he was waiting for me. I shook hands with the professor and noticed something changed in me forever.

Cousin Joannie took a photo of me with my diploma, handed me a check for twenty-five dollars, drove me home, and left to return to her family. I stood staring at my front door, my two roommates and their families abuzz inside with excitement for their sons' graduations. In a chaotic exit, everyone left for a celebratory dinner. I stood in the living room alone, my diploma still in my hand. I fought feeling left behind, invisible again, challenged to matter, again. *This was my day!* I didn't have to give it away if I didn't want to. And I didn't want to. I held the diploma close to my heart. I loved my new self.

Minutes later the doorbell rang, and a guy I had started dating stood before me, the excitement of the day still showing on his face. He had just come from his graduation. UCSC had separate ceremonies depending upon your discipline of study. His family was waiting in the car to take him to dinner, but he had come over to get the present I made for him. He said he loved the quilt, that no one ever made him a quilt before, and left all smiles. He gave me nothing, not even a hug or word of congratulations. He walked to his parents' car, and I watched them drive off and turn the corner.

In my desire to have someone share the good news with me, I called you, fantasizing that, despite our differences, you would at least be glad for me. I couldn't give up on you, Mom. Dad uncharacteristically answered the phone. I kept the fantasy going that you would not let me down, *not today!*

"Hi Dad," I said. "I graduated today."

Silence.

"Huh, so now you think you're smarter than everybody else?"

I held my breath. "No," I said in a barely audible voice. I felt the edge of his shame emerge and it cut through me. I knew his shame well. I spent my life trying not to awaken the beast. I knew when he felt shame he shamed me. I knew better than to believe he meant what he said. I tried to stay compassionate to him and positive for myself.

You lost your dream to be a scientist, and my heart always broke for your broken dreams. I triggered you and Dad. Dad had to give up his dreams to take care of his mother when his dad died, and he was only sixteen. I've analyzed this moment for decades, Mom. I struggled with ungluing myself from the disappointment in your own lives. I had to do that to have my own future. I claimed my right to be deserving. Does that make sense now?

Why was being happy so complicated?

I walked back to the living room and unrolled my diploma. I stared at my name in large letters, and I heard myself say, "I have no regrets."

* * *

After graduation, I began to search for a job. With a degree in philosophy, I had no idea what kind of job would accommodate my need to feel fulfilled. I didn't want to teach, I simply loved studying philosophy. But, now what?

Once again, I relied on my marketable skills. I accepted a job at a law firm in Santa Cruz working for a probate attorney. With four years of college behind me, I found myself feeling as if I had come full circle and was back in a rut. I worked for him for a year. It was a good law firm with good people, but I still wanted to do something else.

I took a job with a title company hoping I would have mobility, perhaps go into management with an opportunity for higher pay. Yes, I was a secretary again but at least in this job I could get promoted into a more lucrative position. No lawyer was ever going to promote me to attorney.

A year after that job, in 1977, I realized if I didn't do something to change my life, again, I'd find myself at fifty doing the same job with the same marketable skills. I panicked. I stared into the redwood forest for a minute to collect myself and see if I could feel a sense of what to do. Then a surge came up through my torso. I knew I had to quit.

I had recently quit having panic attacks. Through writing and meditation, correcting some dysfunctional beliefs about myself, they left one day and never returned. Therapists didn't know about anxiety back then, and no one could help me with it. It was horrible having to go through those attacks. They lasted for seven years. I decided I couldn't let people go through them alone as I had. I wanted to help people with anxiety. The internal knowing was as clear as watching a movie. How was I going to follow this desire? I had no clue.

I never told you about these horrible, paralyzing episodes because I knew I would have made you more anxious than you already were. Mine began when I was twenty-one, when I felt deeply unloved and unwanted. There was one reason for them, but they were triggered by two people. The betrayal I felt from both you and my first love conflated and filled me with shame. Each time I had an anxious episode I felt your suffering too. It was all too much to deal with and I just wanted to hide.

So, on a sunny day, staring into the dense redwoods, I turned off my typewriter, walked into my boss's office, and gave a month's notice. He hadn't expected my resignation since we worked well together. Clearly, I upset him. He offered me a raise and tried to persuade me to stay. But I needed to find a way to feel passionate about what I did every day. This wasn't it.

I wasn't sure what was, but I was certain this wasn't.

I knew I had come a long way but still felt as if I hadn't gone anywhere at all. I thought about going back to school to major in creative writing, and I would have loved that, but I already had school loans, and helping others felt like the right way to go. I knew I'd continue writing, but it wasn't a career choice; helping others would be.

I called a friend and went over to her place on my lunch hour. We looked through the local paper to see what jobs were available. I found an ad for a reading specialist for a new Title XX program designed to help children in kindergarten through second grade raise their low reading scores. I applied. It was a step into the people-helping field and out of being a secretary.

The grammar school scheduled me to come in, and in the

interview the principal asked me what significant event happens in the life of a five-year-old. I made up something I don't remember now, but it wasn't the answer he wanted. The answer he wanted was five-year-olds start school. But I started school at four because my birthday is in November, so the answer he wanted didn't come to mind. The woman in charge of the reading program hired me despite the principal's protests. She later told me she loved my energy and knew I would be good at teaching kids how to read. I never suspected being in remedial reading myself would one day help me help other kids, but it did.

When I started meeting the students I made sure to ask each one about their home life because I suspected it was probably affecting their concentration. Not surprisingly, they each had issues in their family that made them worry about their parents while they were in school. I decided to begin each remedial session by taking the kid out to the playground to throw a ball, or draw, or laugh. After they had some fun and one-on-one time with me, we opened the books. The kids' scores went up several grades. We were all pleased. It taught me what kids are capable of when they are feeling good. They needed to use their minds for things other than worrying about grownups. Don't we all do better when we feel loved and are able to think about what we are doing in the moment?

Unfortunately, a year later Title XX lost funding, and I lost my job. You were still alive at the time, but I couldn't tell you because I never would have heard the end of it.

I lived in a hundred-year-old water tank, and I loved it. I rented it from a friend. It had a large yard with fragranced tea roses and sweet blackberries growing up a fence. The building was tiny, with a little loft for my mattress.

The rent for this little beauty of a home was $140 in 1977. Now here's the ridiculous part, Mom. I was only making $220 at the school. Money was tight, as you might guess, but I made it work because you showed me how to manage money. I never went hungry. I always paid my bills on time. And I was still okay without all the convenient and luxurious things my friends had. I never allowed myself to feel jealous. Jealousy is a toxic emotion. If I spent my time working for what my friends had, I never would have gotten through those lean times, and I might never have had the motivation to move on with my life's dreams.

During this time, while at a club with my friend Jenny listening to Neil Young sing, I met a man and started dating him. He lived up in the mountains. After a year, we both got an eviction notice within the same month. We didn't know what we were going to do. He had a full-time job, but I was about to be unemployed. I don't think either one of us thought moving in together was the right move, but it was convenient and timely, so we did. We rented a little Victorian a few blocks from the ocean. It was a wonderful house. At night I could hear the seals bark, the people on the roller coaster scream with fright, and the foghorns belt out their song in the early morning hours.

During a full moon, I drove a few blocks to watch its light melt into the ocean waves. It was mesmerizing, uplifting, emboldening, and it gave me the peace I needed to think, because our relationship brought me great distress. As perfect as everyone thought he was, at home he wouldn't communicate about anything of significance; there was no room to discuss emotions, plans, or dreams, and he didn't seem to have an interest in getting to know me.

I hadn't expected our relationship to be so difficult. It was tough. He had no aspirations, resisted with all his might against any form of change, good or not so good. I tried to change his belief about change, because how could you survive life without a philosophy about change? Life with him had to go his way or he became shaming. You can imagine how that didn't work for me. No amount of reasoning got through to him. He was paralyzed with the fear of making a mistake and struggled to be perfect. He had such a grip on daily life, I began having health issues again.

When I couldn't change him, I tried to change me so I could be at peace with his belligerence, but I couldn't do that either. I wasn't afraid of change, but I was afraid of changing myself if the only reason was to accommodate dysfunction. I wanted progress, improvement, a deeper commitment. His mother was a huge obstacle. She didn't like the fact that I came from Brooklyn, she didn't like the fact that Nana was Puerto Rican, and quite basically, she didn't like anything or anyone who got in the way of her controlling her grown son.

I tried talking to you about it a few times, but you just went to your own pain, and I didn't think that helped either of us. Instead, I picked up my journal, wrote letters to God and entered a place of solace.

My boyfriend had demands on me. You had demands on me. I couldn't accommodate each of you without giving up on me in ways that made me terribly unhappy, not because I didn't want to please either of you, but because neither of you seemed to care about me. Then I stopped talking to both of you about my unhappiness and decided to take action to make my life better. I knew my days were numbered with him.

TWENTY-NINE

I interviewed with a group home and was hired. It was a residential treatment center for children ages five through eighteen who needed help after being released from NAPA State Hospital or juvenile probation in the state of California. Teens were your favorite people, and I remember how you fought the church to keep the recreation hall open on Fridays so the teens in church could have someplace to go besides bars and dark streets at night. You would have loved these teens, Mom. I certainly did. I could feel the power of your influence working through me. So many people had given up on these kids, but I didn't. I loved working with them, challenging as they were.

On one of my visits home, I attempted to share this job with you. I thought we could share our mutual love for teens, but you got angry and upset. You stomped upstairs, leaving me in mid-sentence. I sat on the couch choked up, wondering what the hell happened to set you off so strongly. I was so sure my exciting job was an opening for us to share, to bond over mutual interests, not to be pulled apart. You didn't speak about why you got upset when you reentered the living room, and I was fearful of bringing it up.

I worked for the agency for a few months, then decided I wanted to go to grad school for social work. I told my boyfriend I was applying to San Jose State.

He said, "Well, I'm not going to help you."

"Well, I'm going. You can help me or not." I left the room more determined than ever.

The job was stressful and demanding. Sometimes the teens attacked the staff, so I joined a health club and began lifting weights to become physically stronger. The female staff began talking about the discrimination between how the agency treated the male staff versus female staff. It was a tough job. We had twenty-four-hour shifts. Men knocked the kids to the floor and restrained them, the teens kicking and screaming until they fell asleep. The women did not have the same physical strength, so we had to be creative, find ways to distract them or keep them calm by talking to them to find out why they were triggered. Female staff got no help. If we couldn't physically knock them to the floor and restrain them, we wouldn't be doing our jobs. What a lousy way to help kids with mental health and emotional problems. I couldn't stand what I saw, and the entire female staff decided to talk to state licensing. I admit, I was the leader of this mini revolt.

Meanwhile, I applied to a local hospital's in-patient program thinking I would switch from kids to adults; plus it was only ten minutes from home instead of forty. My application for the adult in-patient unit went without an interview; they weren't hiring so I forgot about it.

Meanwhile, San Jose State University accepted my application for my master's in social work. My boyfriend and his mother tried to talk me out of it. They said I shouldn't have a degree higher than him. Not a very good reason to deter my dreams and I certainly, by this time, was too smart to fall for that one. Although he made it as tough on me as possible, I kept going. I was writing prayers to God nightly to give me enough strength to get through over two hours of daily driving, working long shifts and school assignments. The relationship was hurting me in so many ways and at the time your anger was accelerating too, Mom. You didn't seem to want me to go back to college either. I had opposition from all sides.

The only good thing about the job was they agreed to sponsor hours for school credits, enabling me to work and go to school. My shifts were changed to graveyard shifts, and I managed to do most of my homework when the kids slept, that is, if I didn't fall asleep too. I was busy seven days a week and I would be for two years, but I made a commitment to my future and dug in my heels. Or as you would say, I pulled myself up by my bootstraps.

Meanwhile State Licensing agreed to meet with the female staff. They listened to our experiences of working there. The horrified look on their faces revealed how they felt about what we were relaying to them. Just as the first year of school ended and I was asked to do an internship at Los Gatos County Mental Health, State Licensing closed the group home. I looked to my boyfriend for comfort but the distress between us was making me sick. My endometriosis had become so painful, there were days I couldn't stand up straight. Despite being in a relationship, I felt more isolated than ever as he put all his energy into his job which only made me more alone.

One spring day as I stared out our back window, I noticed the bulbs I had planted five years earlier had begun to break ground. Every spring I told myself things would get better between us, but they didn't. What is the point of having a significant other if you aren't significant? I wrote more letters to God and asked him to help with the needed funds to get me out of the relationship. I feared I would die of loneliness. Attempted conversations with him were killed on the spot with him shaming me, disqualifying my experience, and letting me know he was not going to share the control of our relationship. He was purely a dictator.

Then my graduation day from San Jose State arrived. I shouldn't have been surprised or hurt, but I was. There was no statement of congratulations, no gift, not even a dinner out in a nice restaurant. For two years he had watched me work and study full-time. He had watched me fight fatigue with school and work. He had watched my endometrial pain worsen. He watched. But that's all he did.

The day of my graduation I refused to let his jealousy over my accomplishment affect me. His parents drove us to the ceremony. His mother and I sat in the backseat. She handed me a card with a check for twenty-five dollars and proceeded to tell me how she did the right thing by leaving her career for her husband and I should be doing the same for her son. I watched my boyfriend staring straight ahead in the front seat. He didn't look back at me. He didn't tell his mother to stop. He didn't say a word.

I wanted to be taken out for a celebratory dinner, but the plans were prearranged by my boyfriend and his mother. We were having dinner at their home. His dad was excited about my graduation and took photos of me in his rose garden and other places where flowers were blooming. He was a tough man, but we had a meeting of the minds early on and we got along great. He was so caring and kind to me. Once when his son and I went skiing, I left my VW in his driveway. When I returned, I noticed he had replaced the tires on my car. I did so much driving while going to school and work, I hadn't noticed that the treads on my tires were bare.

Just as I graduated from San Jose State, President Reagan cancelled funds designated for mental health services, and it took me nine months to find a job. I could have gotten a better one outside Santa Cruz, but my boyfriend would not move away from his mother, and I didn't have the money to leave town alone, so I hung in there.

Mom, remember when I called you to help me the last three months of the program? I only needed ninety dollars a month to make it. I couldn't work and finish my thesis. I only had three months left. *Three!* I asked my boyfriend for the money. He just shook his head and that was that. I know he thought if he didn't help me financially I'd have to quit school, but I wouldn't do it. I refused. For the next three months you sent me ninety dollars, albeit with a guilt trip for taking your cigarette money. But I was deeply grateful to you, Mom. Thank you so much. You came through when it really mattered, and I had no other resources.

After all the managing I did to get out of grad school to find a job where I could earn enough money to set out on my own, I couldn't believe I then had nine months of unemployment due to our government's refusal to fund mental health programs.

Again, I had to resort to my skills. I found a legal secretary job in Monterey for a one-man law firm whose secretary was on medical leave. I also crocheted bathing suit tops, sewed sun dresses, skirts, slacks and sold them on consignment in local stores. My goal now was money. Bring in the money!

About nine months later one of my colleagues called. She was in a car accident and had to quit. Did I want her job? An hour away from home, but I took it. It was a therapist position for another group home. I made a decent salary, but I still needed more if I wanted to move out and live on my own.

Here is another God intervention, Mom.

Remember I said I had sent a resume to an adult inpatient mental health unit, but they weren't hiring? Well, that resume was, unbeknownst to me, redirected to a new Employee Assistance Program the local hospital was developing, and they wanted me to come in for an interview. They hired me in the interview to work four hours a week. I went to my supervisor and asked if I could have Friday mornings off for the job. Without question, he said he had no problems with it because I had good management skills, and my court reports and probation reports were always completed a week in advance.

Now I had two jobs. I saved the salary from the part-time job and as much as I could from the full-time job, enabling me to design a plan to leave my dead-end relationship. I wanted to give my boyfriend one more chance to decide if he wanted our relationship to go forward or not. Don't ask me why I made such a stupid decision, but I did. I knew I needed to leave and there was no expectation he would do a full 180. I knew he wouldn't and couldn't do that. But I couldn't help but offer the last olive branch on the darn tree. I loathed myself for making such a gesture. What if he took it? What if he said, yes, he wanted to change, then what? Would I give it to him, knowing how many seconds the changes would last? He just liked jerking me back and forth to see what control he had over me. Would I really be so stupid as to stay just to feel *nice*? Doubts, they're dangerous. Believing I had to be "nice" was even more dangerous.

It was at this time that something happened to change my life forever.

THIRTY-THREE

Remember Christmas 1983, when my boyfriend and I went back to New York for Christmas to visit you and Dad? That was a traumatic time for me. Not because you were still angry with me, but because I saw how much your health was failing. I was shocked at your appearance, Mom. Dad looked more stressed than I'd ever seen him. The way he looked at you, as if you had already died, grief already on his traumatized face.

Your once beautiful, well-curved gams swollen and gray. Your toes hardly fit into your shoes. Your skin gray as ash. I wanted to throw my arms around you, sob in your lap, hold you tight and give you some of my breath to make you live longer, but I knew you wouldn't like that. You didn't like it when I "hung" onto you, as you always called any form of touch. If you hadn't trained me not to touch you, trust me, I would have done just that. This was the defining moment, Mom. We could have turned everything around in this two-week visit.

I wanted you to go to the hospital for help. You said you didn't want to go to the hospital because grandma died in one. Did it make more sense to die at home when you could have gotten help at the hospital?

Dad walked around the corners of the rooms fearing he would find you lying on the floor dead. I saw his panic and I started feeling it too. You were still crocheting baby clothes as if

I were already pregnant. Even in your last days you couldn't let go of the need to remind me you had no grandchildren. Didn't your jaw hurt clenching it so tightly each time you spoke to me?

I knew every time I looked at you I would never see you again. I kept trying to figure out a way to turn it all around. What could I say to help you save us? I came up with nothing, Mom. You had taken away all my ideas, even throwing the bag of malted milk balls I bought to soften your anger across the room. Was nothing sacred anymore?

The day we were to head back to California, you sat in the green chair in the living room biting your nails. Dad and my boyfriend waited in the car while I anxiously walked toward you to find a way to say goodbye. My feet felt like cement, heavy and taking what seemed like a long time to walk the three yards from the stairs to the green chair you sat in. Ever mindful that Dad was waiting, and he hated waiting. Pinched between wanting to hurry for him and wanting to take my time to say the right thing to you because this was my last chance, I walked over to you and threw my arms around you.

Do you remember what you did? This was my last moment with you forever and you started punching me lightly on the back, repeating, "Janet, you're hurting me. Janet, you're hurting me." I knew I wasn't because I barely touched you. I didn't want to let go until you stopped punching so I could take home a touch of your arm, but you wouldn't stop, and dad was waiting, and I knew I had to go. I just wanted one soft touch mom, just anything—anything tender.

I don't remember the drive to the airport or even saying goodbye to Dad. I knew once he got in the car alone, he would cry all the way home. And I felt ripped in half. I wanted to take a cab back to you, stay another week and force the issue, but I knew it would only make things worse and I had to go back to work the next day. I hated what I was feeling, yet I had no way to fix any of it.

Once on the plane, I told my boyfriend you weren't going to live long enough to see your birthday on the seventeenth of February. He told me what he always told me: I was wrong and not to make a big deal out of it. I ignored him. I wasn't going to argue. I knew what I knew.

February fifteenth, 3:00 a.m., the phone rang. My boyfriend shook me awake. I struggled out of a deep sleep. Groggy and confused, I tried to free myself from a dream, my blue flannel nightgown suffocating me with its warmth.

"Your mother died," he said. I tried to sit up; his words became hot arrows. My mind wrestled to be in the moment. I swung my feet around to get out of bed, but the floor was gone. I stood anyway and floated to the back of the house, went outside, and stepped into the dark, cool, ocean fog. A dim light from somewhere was caught in the fog's grip. I must have grabbed the sponge off the kitchen sink on my way out because I was leaning over our rusted garbage can wiping it with force.

"Honey," I heard from the doorway, "what are you doing?"

I looked up and saw my boyfriend at the open door.

"I'm washing the garbage cans. I must do something, or I'll die too."

The words had no vibration inside my mouth. I barely heard them. I was set on "desperate" and had to move. I was pushing my arms through concrete and I couldn't let it harden with me in it. I was fighting for survival. I could easily have vanished with you, Mom. I looked up at my boyfriend, still waiting in the doorway.

I felt the sponge drop from my fingers and saw myself walk up the concrete steps. I followed him into the living room and walked towards our new white couch. I crawled onto it, tucking my feet under my body, and stared out the bay window into pure darkness. I was being swallowed whole. I disappeared.

Sounds from the bedroom caught my attention. My boyfriend was snoring. He wasn't a snorer. I knew his avoidance techniques. Snoring to make believe he was sleeping was one of them. The darkness swallowed me whole again. I lost form.

What's the first thing any daughter wants to do the moment she hears tragic news? *Call her mother!* I wanted to call you; let you know I had just lost my mom. I wanted to hear you tell me everything would be okay. I felt an urgent need to call you— *now!* How was I ever going to make peace with you, without you? I stared into my irreparable, permanent, devastating new reality.

I had heard your aphorism dozens of times: "Janet, always be prepared." How could I prepare for a life without you? I had a medicine cabinet prepared for accidents and illnesses. I had a toolbox filled with tools in case I needed them. I had a closet full of clothes for any weather event. But I wasn't prepared for a life without you. How does a daughter prepare for such a thing? How in the world could I be numb and in excruciating pain at the same time? So, tell me, Mom, how could I be prepared for your death?

There was something else that night I could never have suspected I needed to be prepared for: My boyfriend giving me the news my mother died and then going back to bed. *He went back to bed!* Perhaps I didn't notice it at the time, because his neglect and lack of attention towards my distress was toxically familiar. I hadn't questioned it in the beginning of our relationship. Perhaps it was too familiar. My emotional distress was one thing you didn't pay attention to either, Mom. My safe place with you was to simply be dutiful.

Couldn't he have guessed I needed a compassionate touch, a cup of tea, a tissue, a light, his presence next to me, reassurance that I would be okay? He could have asked if I needed anything. How could he not see I had broken into a million pieces?

I didn't move all night, not because I didn't want to go back to bed, but because I couldn't find my body to get me there. I didn't cry. I didn't move. I don't even know if I blinked.

> The moon broke apart
> I lost half of it
> Which part was me?

The light appeared on the street without my notice, and my neighbors began to drive away in their cars in preparation for a new day. How would I prepare for my new day? I wanted to get to New York fast. I had to buy an airline ticket, two tickets. Of that there was no doubt.

I walked to the bathroom and found my boyfriend sitting on the edge of the bathtub hyperventilating. Instead of making the call to the airlines for me, for us, he looked up at me and declared, "You need to take care of me because I've never seen a dead person before."

I came apart at the seams, shouting, "It is *my* mother who died. You will have to take care of *me*." My body shook. A minute before, I was ready to collapse on the floor in tears, now I was ready to put that energy into a fight. It was the only thing that held me up while I tried to wrap my mind around his selfishness.

Why did his response surprise me? Hadn't he always told me during difficult times he would not help me? Didn't he always chant he didn't want any woman dependent on him for anything? Didn't he realize he had a daily dependence on me to make him look as if he had it all together?

I called the airlines and explained through gasps that I needed to make two immediate plane reservations. I tried to control my impulse to sob to this caring ticket agent who gave me her condolences. My "partner" was in the next room, but I was on an island.

We headed for the airport as soon as we could. I thought of Dad. Dad holding in tears. Dad reaching for a beer. Dad waiting for me. Dad not knowing what to do. Dad in great suffering. Dad pacing. Dad with no patience and no way to calm down because that was your job. How would I comfort him when I needed comforting too? I braced myself for all the emotions that would be swirling around us with no way to deal with them except exploding at one another.

My attention was drawn to a man at the front of the plane making squeaking sounds with colorful balloons as he twisted them into animal shapes. I wanted to scream at him to sit down, he agitated me, and I became fearful he was delaying us from getting off the ground. A flight attendant tried to settle him and get him seated. I thought of your sense of humor and how you must have planned this. It was just like you to arrange such a distracting funny situation. The man continued blowing up the long colorful balloons and squeezing them into dogs and cats, handing them out to passengers. He came my way, but I turned my head, not wanting to engage him. As strange as this sounds, I didn't want to feel better. I needed to stay ensconced in my grief, to hold it, to feel its heavy stance in my heart, I didn't want to lighten the feeling. I didn't want you to disappear. You were that grief. It was all I had of you now.

Once we landed, we took a cab into Brooklyn. Dad met us at the door. I ran and threw my arms around him and his desperate grief stabbed through me. So much of it is a blur now. That week, not one of us was able to cope with anything. Dad wouldn't talk. He insisted on separating himself from everyone, refusing to express his emotions. I didn't know what to do at dinner. Should I sit in your seat? Would we be able to stay at the table with the chair empty? I felt responsible for filling your absence because, well, wasn't that my job? I asked Dad if he wanted me to sit in your chair at the opposite end of the table from him and he went pale. I pulled out the chair and waited, then realized I couldn't look at an empty chair and sat. Oh Mom, I died a million deaths those few days. I walked around the funeral home like a zombie. We all did.

Dad said he didn't want to bury you on your birthday, and I nodded in agreement. He said he wanted to sell the house fast because he couldn't deal with all the memories. I asked him to wait two years. Although I understood wanting to run from memories—I did it myself when I left for California—I knew he wouldn't be able to deal with living in an apartment after owning his own home. I told him he didn't want to regret a decision like that and he should wait. He dropped his head down and agreed. He was suffering so deeply it was difficult to sit next to him, yet I wanted to move closer just the same.

We held your services over for an additional night and buried you on the eighteenth. I anxiously awaited the arrival of the birthday present I had sent you and found it by the back porch door. I quickly took it upstairs so Dad wouldn't see it and hid it in my luggage. I was so glad I found it before he did.

I sat with him a lot during your funeral services. His grief was awful to watch. I had seen him in pain before, but never like this. He was a wounded lost duck.

On your birthday, the funeral parlor was standing room only. Really, Mom, the line was out the door. I would have sung you "happy birthday," but I couldn't get my voice to work. I couldn't get my legs to work. I sat in a state of lost identity, my voice gone, my sense of self hanging above me where I couldn't reach it. I should have bought you balloons for your birthday, but I didn't think of it. I was living in a traumatized numbness and I couldn't stay present. I kept watching my boyfriend to make sure he didn't piss Dad off. I kept reaching out to Dad, following him around to make sure he was okay. Of course he wasn't, but I needed to sit with him just in case he needed to say something.

Uncle Harold was devastated and pulled a rose from a wreath standing by the door. He placed it on your chest, and I did the same, pricking my finger and watching it bleed, yet not feeling it.

Dad kept asking everyone, "Doesn't Ruthie look beautiful? Doesn't she look beautiful?" I was glad he thought so, but it made me angry. Why didn't he tell you that when you were alive? I know it would have meant so much to you. I was tempted to remind him of that, but there was no point. I watched his guilt rise and his drinking increase, and there was nothing I could say that would help. If I brought up a memory, he'd shout at me not to talk about it.

I rummaged through photographs and pasted them into an album. When Dad got home from work, I showed it to him, excited to go through it with him and remember. I simply wanted someone to remember with. But he just yelled at me to stop talking about it and left the room. I couldn't talk to anyone about my grief. No one wanted to grieve with me. I was outside my skin watching myself drift further and further away.

I slipped a card into your casket. I hope you understood it. I hoped you knew it was written in love for both of us. I never meant for my life to hurt you.

I knew very few people at your funeral. You'll love this one, Mom. I went up to one of the women in the crowded room and asked her how she knew you. She smiled and said she met you at the bus stop. *At the bus stop!* Only you could make friends at a bus stop and make such an impression upon them they show up at your funeral!

I stared at your face for a long time, wanting to sear it into my memory. Not that I would ever forget you, but I was afraid the day would come when maybe I wouldn't be able to recall your face. Did you worry about that when Grandma died? Anyway, I stared at the purple mole on your right cheek and realized I would never see that mole again. I remembered you told me not to squeeze a pimple because that is how the purple mole came about.

Shortly after we buried you, I looked in the mirror and there it was! That purple mole. There it was, on my left cheek. Did you send it to me? Silly question. But I have it now forever, Mom. On my left cheek. Forever.

I had been seeing a therapist who helped me with some of my feelings about our issues. He had me play in a small sandbox with different objects and figures. It's called sand tray therapy, and therapists do it with kids. He asked me to select an object that symbolized you. I chose a golf-ball sized crystal. I bet you're surprised at that, but it is true. I bet you thought I would select a rubber chicken or pot or maybe a broom.

HOW MUCH CAN A HEART TAKE?

I have become
An island
An orphan
Seeking a continent

Dreams, powerful dreams
Push with whichever
Way the wind blows.

salt on
my face
tears
the wind can't dry

What do I do now?
My mother is gone

I look up.

I reach for yesterday
but yesterday has come and gone
ahead is my fragmented heart
where is my needle and thread?

The space I'm in
has no form
no flavors
no fragrances
no affirmations or mottos
to hold me up
or teach me how to
be prepared

In my hands is my blood
my thin body
tattered
splintered
diced.

What do I do now?
My mother is gone.

I look up.

The sky offers
no end
just vastness and I
try not to
dissipate

What do I do now?
My mother is gone.

I am not wearing boots
I have no bootstraps

I look up.
Always, I look up.

What do I do now?
My mother is gone.

My mother is gone.

THIRTY-FIVE

My boyfriend and I went to be with Dad the first Christmas without you. Dad was not doing well. It didn't feel like home without you. There was no clam chowder waiting on the stove for me or an angry mom to contend with. That might have seemed like a relief but surprisingly, it wasn't. There stood that darn empty chair again. There was a litany of absences. There was no coffee smell in the morning from Dad's coffee. There were no familiar sounds, no clanking of pots, no sounds of laughter on the phone with your friends, the crisp noises of wrapping paper and scotch tape squealing off its role to wrap Christmas presents. I missed the strangest things. The air held heartbreak. It was unrelenting.

The day we left, Dad stood in the doorway and watched as the cab pulled away from the curb. It broke my heart to see him there alone, waiting for us to leave to have his cry. Oh Mom, you were so very missed.

* * *

Once my boyfriend and I got back to California, I started circling apartment ads to rent and townhouses to buy in the Santa Cruz newspaper. Twelve institutions told me they wouldn't give me a loan because I was single and would someday have a baby and not be able to pay my mortgage. I stood up, grabbed my purse, told them in no uncertain terms that if I had a child, they would still get their money. If I could work my way through six years of college and pay all my bills on time, I could pay a mortgage. I stared down at my feet in my black open-toed shoes and thought of you. You always wore open-toed shoes, and I had taken to them myself. But I wasn't standing in my shoes, Mom, I was standing in yours, and it was your feet I was seeing, and it was your voice I was hearing.

I thought of an associate I worked with at the Title Company, Ron Lyons, who focused solely on helping veterans get loans for homebuying. I told him what I was up against. He said he could help and found a lender who would give me a loan. Dad had to co-sign. He was willing to do that, but he became frantic. He had trouble with the forms and yelled at me that you weren't around to help and he didn't know how to do it.

We found a way to do the paperwork, but Dad could barely think straight without you. He ate out every night for a year. When he decided to learn how to cook, he asked the butcher to help him with a simple recipe. Guess what it was. *Corned beef!* I was so proud of him.

My loan secured, I told my boyfriend my plans to move out, and he went about his days as if I hadn't mentioned anything. I figured it would upset him, so I made sure to keep my blue escrow folder on the seat of my VW Bug until everything was settled. It took nine months for everything to fall into place, and each time he tried to set me up for an argument I reminded him I was on my way out and no longer had an investment in our relationship. I told him I fought for the survival of our relationship for eight years, now we were going to live in peaceful alienation. I didn't argue with him over anything from that moment on. When you aren't invested, there is no point. Not arguing didn't change anything, so I had no regrets. There was nothing more between us to fight for.

Once the sale of the townhouse was finalized, I packed up my things and left.

After I moved out he told me, "I was hoping your loan would fall through so you would stay with me."

"You still don't get it," I retorted. "If my loan had fallen through, I would have rented an apartment. I gave you eight years, that's enough."

His face froze.

For the first three months after I left, I'd come home to find flowers, wine, shells, or other trinkets at my door. He said he wanted to take me to dinner to talk. He never wanted to talk when we were together, but suddenly he was interested in talking. I agreed to have dinner and knew there was no way I would sell my new townhouse and move back with him. I had made peace with him in my heart. I was determined not to carry anger, regret, sadness, or longing into my future.

He took me to my favorite seafood restaurant on the wharf and I waited for him to say what he wanted to say. He said his mother hadn't realized he would be so depressed without me, and she wanted to help him woo me back. I listened in utter disbelief. For eight years—just as I thought—his mother had pulled the reins, and she still was. When mothers won't let their kids go, lives get ruined. He could never stand up to her. He would never defend me from her. We had more fights about his lack of courage with her.

I thought of all the arguments we had over eight years about his mother's interference and his inability to stand up to her. What could I say that would make him realize it was far too late to open a conversation about this? I took a breath and waited.

"Tell your mother she can have you now."

* * *

That was an important time for me, Mom, leaving an emotionally distraught relationship, getting my graduate degree, buying a house, pursuing and understanding what it meant to have spiritual fulfillment. I was thirty-four and I had entered a new and challenging chapter of my life.

* * *

You always understood my prophetic dreams because you had them too. Remember you had the dream about Grandma climbing a ladder to heaven and the next day she died? When I first left home and started my life in California, I hated that my hands, feet, fingers and laugh resembled yours. I wanted to know who I was separate from you. I felt separate from you, I wanted to *be* separate from you. As the years went on, and certainly after your death, resembling you made me realize how impossible it would be to ever be totally independent from you. We are one and two at the same time. I've made peace with it.

* * *

I couldn't write a word in my journal for the first year after your death. I couldn't face that you were really gone. I kept telling myself that it was common to have periods of your painful silent treatments. To write would have broken apart the delusion I needed to still hold onto.

I felt as if I were wrapped in Styrofoam. I couldn't awaken from feeling numb often wondering if I'd ever get back to myself again. I knew I had to start writing. I knew it was the only way back. My body held a punching ache from head to toe, my bones hurt, my nerves were taut, my muscles were exhausted from carrying the weight of grief.

On that first anniversary date of your death, I finally opened my journal, took out a pen and wrote. I don't know what I wrote or how long I wrote, but I sat there until I emptied myself. I wasn't just grieving you; I was grieving the relationship we never had. Oh Mom, don't you wish we could do it all over, have more time to work things out? Don't we always think we have enough time? Well, I thought so. I never allowed myself to doubt we would somehow, someday tie up all the situations that hurt for so long and tuck them into an envelope marked "paid."

How many times can a daughter swallow herself up and not have it manifest somewhere? I think it manifested in my handwriting. I noticed after you died the words with the letter "i" in them were written without the "i." It took me awhile to realize it was only the "i" I was leaving out. In so many ways, you were a bigger force in our relationship because, after all, you were the mom. But as I grew up, I was still treated as a child and felt left out of the grown-up relationship it was time for, and for which I was ready. So, I guess it wasn't surprising that the letter "i" was organically left out of my written words. Symbolic, huh Mom?

THIRTY-EIGHT

A recurring dream forced me awake. I dreamt someone had cut off my thigh-length hair and I reached for it, making sure it was still there.

I could not shake this dream. In fact, my thick hair had been thinning for some time, and I was concerned it lacked enough nutrients. One day at work, I mentioned my concern about my hair to my secretary. A few days later, she brought in a well-known health magazine advertising a nurse in Oklahoma who performed hair analyses. I contacted the woman, eager to find help. I sent her a lock of my hair, roots attached as instructed, and waited.

A few weeks later I received a bag of herbs. The ingredients list for the herbal formula was not on the bag and I almost didn't take them. But I was anxious to get my thick hair restored, so I made the tea as instructed and drank it for four days.

I had just started dating a man, and as I finished the four days of herbal tea, he picked me up to show me his place in the Santa Cruz Mountains. It was a stunning area with deep patches of redwood and eucalyptus trees, each fragrant and pungent.

As darkness descended, the sky turned a rich ebony, making it easy to see each star. My boyfriend showed me the tiered vegetable garden he and his roommates had just built and filled with flowers and veggies. I got comfortable on his deck as he went inside to make a pot of peppermint tea. The night was warm, and as I looked up, I saw two shooting stars skim across the sky. It was the first time I had seen shooting stars, and it was magical. I called out to him to come see, but by the time he got out there the show was over. The night felt perfect, peaceful. It was exactly what I needed after a rough week of counseling delinquent teens. I got up to use the bathroom and just as I was about to sit, I felt an unexpected quick movement, as if my head and shoulders were being pulled in separate directions like returning a carriage on a typewriter.

The mirror showed a startled and frightening face, and I heard myself whisper, "God be with me!" Seriously distracted and forgetting to pee, I started to walk back towards the living room. My boyfriend was just about to put the pot of peppermint tea on his table when he looked at me.

I asked, "Did you feel that?" I was hoping the jolting had been an earthquake—a frequent occurrence in Santa Cruz.

He quickly lifted me and carried me to a large pillow. He handed me his phone and said, "Call the hospital."

I worked at the hospital and knew the number, but my fingers couldn't press the buttons, they had become numb and weak, and my knuckles collapsed under pressure.

I barely mumbled the number and watched him dial. He described what he was witnessing to someone who instructed, "Bring her in, now!" If only we had stayed at my place. My townhouse was closer to the hospital, but that night I was forty-five minutes into the mountains off a sharply curved road. Beautiful, but not very convenient at a time like this.

He drove with quick stops and starts, negotiating around the mountain's curves. I started vomiting and passing out. He said he wanted to stop but there was no shoulder, and he also knew he had to hurry. I mumbled to slow down a little and the next time I became conscious he was driving into the hospital driveway looking for the ER, which they had just relocated in the rear of the hospital instead of the front, where it had been since its original construction. I directed him down the long dark driveway. By now it was near eleven.

He ran around and opened the door to help me out of his truck, then began screaming for help, his deep voice echoing in the alley entrance. I started to fall into his arms, barely able to control my muscles. A male appeared in the entrance and pushed a wheelchair towards me, helped me get seated, then rushed the chair through the doors, my boyfriend running behind us.

I mumbled, trying to get someone to give me a pail; I knew I was about to throw up. A nurse handed me a shallow pink bowl in the shape of a smile. I remember thinking, "*If they think that's going to hold my vomit, they are going to be sorely disappointed.*"

I was laid on a gurney and doing what I could to answer the nurse's many questions when I heard myself screaming at the top of my lungs. The nurses ran around not knowing why I was screaming. I was confused. I thought I was talking. The male nurse sat close to me with the most distressed and perplexed look, but I couldn't help him, and it seems he couldn't help me.

I heard the nurse shout that they would have to rush me to Community Hospital because the MRI at Dominican was out of order. The next thing I remember was opening my eyes in time to watch them feed me into a dark tube. When I awoke, I was in an ambulance rushing back to Dominican Hospital, still throwing up all over myself. I tried to lift my head but couldn't and the nurse compassionately accommodated me, wiping my long hair away from my face. He yelled out to the driver, "She's throwing up!" I thought how sweet he was to help me rather than scold me for making a mess in his ambulance. And not just that, I was making a mess all over him. I expected to be yelled at, but he was gentle. Then I disappeared and woke up four days later and during that time, I had the following dream:

I was in the dark sky with you, Mom, and Emily (my boyfriend's roommate who was killed by a drunk driver a few weeks before), sitting on kindergarten chairs with no floor underneath us. I asked both of you if I should come back to my body. I was quite distressed and didn't know what to do. There was no conversation that I remember, just my questions and panic and the two of you sitting with me.

When I awoke, my boyfriend was sitting by my side. I made every effort to tell him about the dream. I couldn't really talk but I didn't realize it. I made gruff, bark-like sounds. Paying close attention, he finally got some of what I was trying to say and reminded me Emily was dead. I tried to tell him I knew that, but it was you I wanted to tell him about, Mom. I had never met Emily. Why she appeared in the dream I have no idea. It was sitting with you that left me panicked and distressed.

One morning I awoke to a red halo. It was my nurse with a head of vibrant red hair, cranking up the bed while declaring she liked her patients to sit up when they were on a feeding tube. *What?* I wanted to ask her what she was talking about, but I couldn't move my lips.

Then my repetitive disturbing dream of having my hair cut made sense as nurses and my neurologist started telling me I had to cut my hair. I moved my eyes back and forth. *"NO!"* Trying to accommodate my wishes, nurses and friends tried to save my hair, rubbing the entangled ball with peanut butter and olive oil, stabbing at strands with a long-tailed comb trying to extricate individual hairs. It was becoming clear what a futile task it was, and I was tired of sleeping on a ball of hair that reeked of peanut butter and oil. Finally, a friend dropped a yellow phone book on my lap and opened it to a page of hairdressers. "Pick one," she said. "The doctor wants you to cut your hair."

The hairdresser showed up, cut off the basketball-sized knot of hair and put it on my lap to show me what a mess it was. What a nest! My friends wanted to know if they should save it for me. How sweet . . . but no. What was I going to do with it now that it wasn't on my head? This was an unbelievable experience, Mom but there is another part of this experience I must share with you.

Shortly after waking up from the coma, I witnessed many figures standing like paper dolls in silky blue spirit forms around the front of my bed. They had no real human characteristics such as eyes, noses, hair, or arms. They were a lovely sight, so calming. They emitted a blue energy of love and peace that encircled my belly button and spread out as large as a dinner plate. I became a pure spirit, no body, no paralysis, no distress, just pure, whole, healthy peace. One of the figures I identified as Sri Yukteswar, and one of them was you, Mom. The other six or seven were a mixture of male and female energies, although I had no sense of who they were. It was comforting to feel you in the room standing before me. A thin silver thread connected all of us to each other through our belly buttons, as if we were one huge soul network.

* * *

I was at Dominican Hospital three weeks, then went to a rehabilitation center for another three weeks. I was supposed to stay there six months, but there was no way I was going to do that. I implemented every healing technique I had learned after I became a therapist. I meditated, even though my brain was injured, disallowing my mind to concentrate for long periods of time. I repeated affirmations about what I would soon be able to do that I couldn't but needed to, and I visualized everything I wanted to do that the doctors said I would never do again: run, walk steady on my feet, work, live alone again. Their prognosis for me was grim, and I wouldn't hear of it.

I told the neurologist at the rehab center I was getting out of their facility as soon as I could. I made deals with him to eat real food and to practice swallowing so I could get the feeding tube removed. I instructed his staff to give me a vacuum and mop and bucket. After all, I set my mind on going home, so I needed to retrain my body to do the things I needed to do at home, not the tasks they wanted me to do, like picking up disks on a tabletop. I needed to learn I could step into a bathtub and walk up a curb and wash a dish. The doctor, Dr. G, accommodated me. He was such a blessing, and I felt safe asking him to help me with how I wanted to recover.

I yelled at the ceiling for you, Mom. The neurologist brought me medical decisions I just wasn't sure how to make. I needed you. You would have been good at helping me with this and with all the difficult decisions I had made over the years, this time I was in over my head. I knew what I wanted the outcome to be but first I had to deal with medical tests, some of which I just knew weren't right for me. I fired one neurologist who had no patience for my distress. When Dr. G arrived, he asked me to close my eyes and the first answer I heard would be the right one. I said 'no' to the angiogram everyone told me I had to have. Dr. G respected that. To jump ahead here a little, a few months later, it turned out, I didn't need it.

I worked hard and it paid off. I never stopped telling the staff what I needed to learn. I asked a nurse to come into my room by six each morning and teach me how to walk to the bathroom. I was not going home in a wheelchair. At first my body flailed in spasms as I tried to take a step. After a couple of weeks, I was able to calm my arms and walk without too much threat of conking her on the head as she held my waist. I left the rehabilitation center three months later instead of the expected six.

I spent a year on disability getting my muscles back in shape, my emotional lability under control, and my spiritual development into perspective. That near-death experience changed my life. Recovering made for a busy year. I worked with my friend, Chris, who spotted me at the gym, and a famous local channeler, who helped me with my emotional lability and sudden ability to see waves of energy inside and being emitted from people. I found I could diagnose bodily distresses, not in the way of a medical diagnosis, but in the way of what the energy was doing in their bodies. I could see the energetic motion and hear its sound, with an accompanying taste and smell at times. In one of the channeler's classes I saw into a woman's chest and told her I witnessed tiny white lights peeking out from the darkness ensconcing her breasts. The light was trying to become brighter. She stared at me for quite a while, then told me she had breast cancer. I cried all the way home. I wanted to help people, but this didn't seem as if it were a gift; it felt like a curse. I found it extremely exhausting and difficult to be around people because I came to know things about them that I didn't want to. Each time I confirmed these insights with people I was accurate, and it scared me. Too much knowing. But near-death experiences opened people to new dimensions, and now I had to figure out what to do with all this. I felt a deeper responsibility towards everyone I encountered.

During my recovery I questioned the meaning of being a therapist and having lost my ability to speak, and being a writer and having lost my ability to write. I had no answers but had become aware that somehow, sometime, all would be revealed. While I was pondering the impact of my NDE, I had another prophetic dream. I was on the beach with God standing near the edge of the waves, talking, when a gold-domed ashram offshore blew up, pieces of its gold dome flying everywhere. We didn't so much as flinch. I wasn't scared. God looked at me, there were no words. I got the message through his stare that I should stop going to ashrams and instead put my healing in His hands. It was a clear message. I awoke with an altered spiritual direction. I stopped chanting with gurus.

FORTY-EIGHT

It was seven years after my near-death illness, and I was finally working enough hours to keep my life financially solvent. It seemed life was finally establishing another sense of normal. But one day when I went home for lunch, I got a call that Dad died. It was 1995.

I was devastated. My friend, Chris, went home with me because I could not face Dad's funeral alone. When you died, I couldn't write for a full year, afraid of what my pen would disclose. When Dad died, I knew I couldn't handle his death the same way. I took two weeks off work, bought fifty dollars' worth of deli food, laid on my couch, and wrote until I couldn't write anymore.

I wished I could have moved into our family home, but it wasn't feasible, so we had to sell it. It broke my heart. We weren't just selling a house. We were selling the vibrant pink azalea bush Dad planted in our front yard for one of your anniversaries and all his beloved tulips in the back yard. We were giving to another family the energy from all the memories, the celebrations, the over-comings, the family dinners, and yes, even the incessant arguments. When I exited it for the last time, I couldn't look back.

It took me a few weeks to cash the check from the sale of the house. By cashing it, my life was turning a page, an unwanted final page. I took the check to Peter, an investment broker. I decided to replace my ten-year-old furniture and fulfill my long-time dream of remodeling my kitchen and bathroom. I was about to turn forty-eight and thought investing in my dream of a beautiful kitchen and bathroom was a good birthday present.

You might want to order another plate of fries, Mom. We're going to be here for a while.

I hired a local company to design a kitchen and bathroom. I sketched what I wanted then walked my plans over to their office. My dream kitchen had counter-to-ceiling white cabinets, puck lights, two lazy Susans, a few glass cabinet doors, brass and silver hardware, slide-out shelves, and three deep drawers. It was perfect. Six weeks later I had my dream kitchen. It was gorgeous, Mom. You would have loved it. I also remodeled my bathroom and upgraded the rest of the place. I bought new furniture, new carpet, and a tall hutch to hold your cut-glass bowls and other family items my sister didn't want.

With my home almost paid off, my kitchen and bathroom remodeled, enough clothes, all the kitchen items I needed, and two self-published books about to be released, I was pleased with my life. I thought I'd travel, write more books, and work part-time. With a new plan in motion, I was on my way to retiring by the ocean. Again, I started feeling I had overcome my challenges and had created an emotional and physical place I could call home.

I fell in love with the kitchen designer, and we dated for two years. December 23, 1999, he called to ask if I wanted to go to my favorite restaurant for a drink and appetizers. I said yes. I called a few of my friends and told them about our date. They were excited and thought he was going to propose. One friend said we were perfect together. She already bought a dress for our wedding. He picked me up at ten thirty and seemed irritated. I thought he was trying to start an argument. Well, who would have guessed what would happen next.

The night was quite romantic, and it was lovely. The full blue moon was high in the sky, the restaurant twinkled with holiday lights, tall gingerbread houses were displayed in all the corners, and there were many Christmas trees lit as well. The sight walking through the restaurant was stunning. But my expected romantic night was soon replaced by his breaking off our two-year relationship. He admitted he was still too attached to his ex-wife. I gave him my thoughts on the situation, then headed down the dark, steep hill lined with tall eucalyptus trees, only the moon's light filtering through them to help me see where I was going. What was strange, Mom, was that I hated my feet closed in and rarely wore sneakers except for at the gym where they were required. But that night, I uncharacteristically put them on instead of heels. For whatever reason I knew to wear them; it was a good thing I did because I never could have made it down that hill sprinkled with eucalyptus pods in heels. The next day, I drove to a friend's house and spent Christmas weekend with them. Thank God for friends.

I spent that New Year's Eve alone. I was not in the mood to go to loud parties while I was trying to make sense of the ending of that relationship. Everyone was hopeful 2000 would bring new opportunities, and I was too, but 2000 came and went uneventful.

When winter 2001 arrived, something strange happened. I was standing in the kitchen and heard a deep inner voice say:

There's always more!
There's always more!

Stopping for a moment, I shook my head and moved on with my tasks. Three months later, the same voice said the same thing:

There's always more!
There's always more!

Again, I stopped what I was doing, then moved on. A few months after that I heard the voice a third time as I stood in the same spot in the kitchen:

There's always more!
There's always more!

By the third time I was freaked out. Was something terrible going to happen? A fire? A robbery? An earthquake? It was terribly unnerving. All I could do was continue living my life and see what happened. You were the only one I could have talked to about something so weird without thinking I had lost my mind. You always had a sixth sense, and it always proved true. Brace yourself, Mom. This one was unbelievable.

FIFTY

As March 2001 arrived, I began having physical symptoms I could not understand. Terrible headaches, brain fog, forgetfulness, burning lungs, and a stinging tongue were only part of the string of symptoms making my life miserable. My breathing became erratic, and my mood started to have unfamiliar swings.

One morning I couldn't remember where I put my toothbrush. I ran around the kitchen and living room searching for it, then I walked into the bathroom and found it in the cup on my sink. I stared at it. Where else would it be? How could I have been confused about this? I lost my voracious appetite. My sleep was shallow. In the morning, I stopped at the end of my driveway and couldn't decide which way to turn to go to the office. It made no sense. Turning to the right was a dead-end hill.

I went to five medical specialists, traveled up to three hours to meet doctors for consultations. Each said I was the sickest patient they had ever seen, but not one of them had any idea what to do for me. One gave me a nose spray—ridiculous.

The symptoms subsided as I began my day and exacerbated once I got home for the night. How could my home be making me sick? I kept a clean home and had just remodeled two of my rooms.

Just the same, I called a contractor I once hired when I was president of the board for my townhouse association, and he came right over. Glen looked around as if he had already known what it was. He was an international forensic mold specialist. He identified water marks on the beams of my cathedral ceiling. He stated there was water in my ceiling and that mold was the problem. He asked me where in the house I felt the symptoms the most. I recalled when I vacuumed near the walls my symptoms worsened. If my roof was leaking, it would make sense the water was coming down the walls. He said he needed to test inside my walls.

Glen inserted a moisture detector into the walls. The light on this device moved from green to yellow to red. He said there was likely an extreme amount of mold inside my walls. I began to learn more about leaks and mold than I could have imagined.

The homeowners' association had just hired a new management company, and without looking at or testing my place, they told me they would do nothing to help me. I became frantic. There was no way I could live in my newly remodeled home. I had to leave, but how could I do that? Everything I needed for living was in my home. I also had a beloved cat. Was she sick too?

I had a psychotherapy business to manage, clients to see. It was important to keep my life stable and calm. I kicked into gear, sleeping nightly in hotels while Glen had specialists in and out testing everything.

I tried going back to the house to care for my cat and do some computer work. I tried sleeping with a heavy respirator mask, hoping that would buy me some time until I could get the association to do what they needed to do because the roof and walls were their responsibility. When I awoke in the middle of the night with blood on my face, I lost all hope. The expensive mold tests revealed my home was saturated with five molds, including Stachybotris, which was a black mold that killed people and pets. Anything exposed to this mold had to be discarded, including my entire home of new furniture I had just purchased with my inheritance. All my clothes, books, everything—a wasteland. Beyond the association policies, I was hurt and confused over why the nine owners and residents would turn so furiously against me when it was clear I needed their help with the building. We had all gotten along. Some I considered friends.

One hot afternoon, I drove to an emergency clinic, but no one would see me. It was flu season, and the clinic was full. I went back to my car, the hot sun baking through my windshield, and faced my worst fear: I was homeless. I had no one to turn to and nowhere to go. I went to Kmart, bought a few plastic cartons, filled them with shampoo, toothpaste, toothbrush, socks, nightgown, underwear, shoes, whatever I thought I would need for daily survival, and organized the trunk of my car the way I had organized my closets.

A few days later I found myself at the Dominican Hospital's Chapel. I sat quietly while others prayed for loved ones in the various units of the hospital. I held in the urge to fall sobbing to my knees. Where was God? I needed Him now. I needed you, Mom. I needed you. If there was ever a time when I would have considered moving back home, this was it. But you and Dad were gone. I signed the hospital's guest book for a prayer for myself, feeling guilty that others were adding prayers for loved ones while I was adding one for myself. There was a statue of Jesus at the door, which I touched, hoping to feel something calming. I wanted to drape myself over it but there was a couple in grief in one of the front pews and I became conscientious about decorum. Imagine that! At a time when I was falling to pieces and wanted to collapse on a statue of Jesus, I was more concerned about a couple in the front row. Even in that intense moment, Mom, I could feel the need to diminish my own suffering for the sake of how others might judge me.

I had to close my business after I sat in front of a long-time client and couldn't remember her name. My life had become a nightmare. For the first time in my life the situation seemed dark, and I couldn't envision what was ahead. I couldn't see a way out. I saw a series of counselors, but not one had a clue about my terror of being homeless and losing everything, including my health and well-planned financial portfolio. No one understood how my life had turned from wellness to destruction, and it seemed the more I talked about the kind of help I needed the more anxious they were to get me to think it wasn't that bad. I didn't need them to minimize my hell, I needed someone to admit it was hell and give me ideas for a resolution. I had become a wanderer in my own town, and I hardly recognized the apathy that came at me from people I knew and trusted. People wanted to know how I caused this. They asked me what I did wrong to have this happen to me. To blame me for this infuriated me. I took better care of my home than my neighbors did, and yet somehow the message was this was my fault.

Mom, my life was uprooted. I had made it a priority to make a place I could call home. In college I moved a lot because I had to. I had paid the price continuing in college demanded. But I had built up my finances, got out of an emotionally tumultuous relationship, bought my own home and created a place to have a settled life. Without a partner, making a home was up to me, and I felt like I had been chasing chariots to do that. It made no sense that I suddenly found myself on the street with nowhere to turn. Then I remembered that voice in my kitchen. The one that repeated:

There's always more.
There's always more.

Is this what that voice meant?

I presented the mold tests to the homeowners' board president and began the remediation at my own expense. I brought in my closest neighbor who bought her place a month before I did. We were original owners and had been there more than fifteen years. She knew I had taken good care of everyone's homes during the years I was president but would not act on my behalf. The remediator told her he wanted me to go to the papers and make a spectacle. He told her there was no reason I should be paying for this work out of my own pocket. This matter, he asserted, was the responsibility of the association and confirmed there was nothing I could have done that would have caused such an issue. I had already paid $18,000 for a small amount of work and there was a lot more to do. He instructed me not to pay a penny more because the board was responsible, and I should sue. I knew the board was responsible, they knew they were responsible, but still they did nothing. I recalled a homeowner meeting years ago when I told the members we had to replace the roofs because a contractor fell through one of them. Had we done that, I wouldn't be in this mess. But all the members voted against it.

I needed a home. My cat needed a home. I missed cooking in my kitchen, sleeping in my bed, working at my computer, and having a roof over my head. I missed my life and nothing was going to bring it back.

One of the homeowners threw her cup of coffee over my new white door. They shunned me when I went back to the house to let contractors and mold specialists in for more testing. One day I sat in the rain on my small lawn, my cat nestled close to my stomach. A homeowner walked by and sneered at me. No one invited me into their homes so I could get out of the rain. No one offered me a cup of tea. I had a bad cold and sat sneezing into a tissue. It was a fierce lesson in non-compassion. In a conversation I had with one of the psychiatrists I referred clients to, he told me we never know the limit to someone's compassion until they are tested. I must admit, I never would have guessed my single, female neighbors would have been so cold-hearted, cruel, or downright evil.

You and Dad always told me people were essentially good. I didn't allow myself to think of anyone as evil, ever, until my friend Charles (who, strangely enough, grew up ten blocks from us in Brooklyn) told me what I was dealing with was pure evil. My reaction was to defend the good of those throwing my life and home into destruction. I found myself saying my neighbors had to have good inside them somewhere.

There is evil in the world, Mom, and it is not just a concept. It lives in real people, like it or not. I liked that you taught me to believe in the good in people, but I also needed to know evil people existed so I would know how to deal with them when I encountered them. I felt unprepared to handle such cruelty. Charles's confidence in their evil turned me around on this issue. I started to believe in the truth of what I was seeing and experiencing and I dropped into deep sadness that I once called these neighbors friends, and now they had become enemies.

I went from one law office to another looking for an attorney. One attorney, a friend of a friend, said he would take the case, but after nine months decided he didn't want to deal with a mold case. I called Erin Brockovich's attorney in LA. He said he would love to take the case, but he would charge a fortune in travel fees. My contractor sent me to his attorney who didn't really want to take the case because there wasn't a large enough payout in it for him, but I went to his office with all my documentation, plopped it on his desk, and asked him if he was bold enough to take on my homeowners' association. He stared up at me and took the case.

It was almost eighteen months before the lawsuit began, and by this time, after many more episodes of heavy rain, the mold had exponentially worsened. Even a ten-minute run to collect papers for lawyers left me sick for weeks. Everything was toxic. Nothing could be removed from my home. Even with a toxicologist and forensic mold specialist's report, the association's lawyers scolded me and threatened to hold me in contempt if I refused to go into my toxic attic for paperwork. I warned them that bringing anything into their offices would contaminate the air in their offices, but they didn't believe me. One day the homeowner association's lawyers went into my home to see for themselves. Neighbors I was still friendly with watched the attorneys in the parking lot gasping and coughing. When I told them what I heard they denied it.

I had to wear a respirator mask in meetings with them when I brought paperwork from my attic. At one point, I got so sick I checked into a hotel and could not move my body. I felt as if something was eating my cells, and I feared for my life. The poisoned feeling is indescribable. I wouldn't wish it on Satan. I couldn't get to the bathroom or to the sink for a glass of water. It felt like I was being eaten alive.

Meanwhile, the remediation company packed my belongings and took them to a storage center. They didn't want to take them to the dump without my approval. Luckily, they chose an outside unit so I could sit outside in fresh air while I went through my possessions for important documents. It was despairing.

The second year of waiting for the association to get off their incompetent butts and do something took an even heavier toll on my immune system. I rented many apartments, but I couldn't stay in them. I kept reacting to smells. Confused about why places with no mold made me sick, I had mold tests performed on each apartment to be sure. Tests confirmed there was no mold. So why was I still having physical symptoms?

Finally, the day came when we met with a judge for the settlement hearing. The judge looked at me and declared with ignorance, "Miss Marquart, I don't believe mold can make you sick. You will not get my sympathy for your case."

I could have gotten up and hit him upside the head. I wanted to dare him to live in my house for one day. I sat there trembling looking like a ninety-year-old woman. My hazel eyes had turned grey, my hair was seriously thinning from the stress, my fingernails were heavily blackened, ridged and curved back into the skin of my fingers, my toenails were black, and I could hardly sit up straight.

When the court settlement was finally over, it was six months before the association was willing to sign the awarded check. They accused me of trying to get rich from the lawsuit. How can you sue yourself and get rich? They had to pass my home to get to their cars. Didn't they notice the remediation work that ensued? Nevertheless, with the small check in hand, I could barely move on. I wanted to keep my home because I had fully reconstructed it. I had put in new hardwood floors, and they were simply gorgeous. However, the thought of being part of such an association disinterested me. I was disgusted not only by their stupidity, arrogance, and lack of compassion, but also by their abuse.

I put my beloved townhouse on the market. My realtor found a new modular home in a park close to the beach. I was on my way to rebuilding my life, or so I thought. Within two days, I started getting a headache. Within two or three weeks, I began reacting with a litany of seriously disturbing symptoms, not the least of which was overpowering brain fog. I had no idea what could be making me sick now. This was a new modular home. It was lovely inside. I kept the windows open with fans blowing, but it made little difference. The longer I stayed in the building the sicker I got until I had to leave, again. My search for holistic doctors and a cure for my distressed body continued.

One day I was out watering the new landscape, and the

president of the townhouse association was driving by slowly, her hyper dog in the front seat. Her window was open, and there I was with a hose in my hand. It was so tempting, Mom. I wanted so badly to aim the hose in her car and drench her for having the nerve to search me out. How dare she! What was she looking for? What did she hope to see? Luckily, I did not stoop to her level or try to get revenge. I watched her drive by. I don't know how she didn't see me, I was standing three feet from her side of the car. Pulling back anger and hate is hard. She was the symbol of all my suffering and loss. I detested her and felt rage at her intrusion. I felt how toxic it was to hate as I watched her drive away, then called my attorney for a restraining order.

Meanwhile my plight to solve the mystery of what was going on in my new home continued. I spoke to many contractors and finally called the remediation company I had worked with to see if they knew what the problem in a new building could be. I explained I was also reacting to car fumes and pesticides from nearby farms and golf courses. I didn't know over-exposure to toxic mold could lead to reactions to other toxins. I moved over twenty times in two years after the onset of getting sick from Stachybotris. I couldn't have imagined what it would do to my health going forward.

The remediator listened with compassion. He said he had seen cases like mine before with some of his other customers and that I had Multiple Chemical Sensitivity, or MCS. I had no idea what MCS was, but I knew I had to find out. My obsessive research began. Not one doctors knew what to do with my symptoms.

Meanwhile, I tried to correct the issues in my new home, replacing carpets with tile and vinyl with hardwood. Then I landscaped my yard with fragrant jasmine and honeysuckle. I bought expensive air filters and wiped down all the walls. But, within two weeks after completely furnishing it with sofas and other items, I began to have serious physical reactions. I discovered there was a high amount of formaldehyde and other chemicals in modular homes. And, my new furniture filled with polyester, nylon, and acrylic, was made with formaldehyde and other toxic chemicals as well. My life was not just chaotic, it had become a spiral of tornados.

Many of my friends had had enough, and they began to end our friendships. They said my mystery illness stressed them out. Since the doctors didn't know why I was sick, everyone concluded I must be crazy. I knew I wasn't crazy. I was desperately ill. Then I met one woman who revealed to me she had MCS too and she settled for living in her apartment without ever going out.

I wasn't going to stifle my life. I went in search of diets, supplements, organic products, natural housing materials. It consumed me. I wanted to get back into the swing of life just as I fought paralysis when the doctors told me all the things I would never do again. I had conquered paralysis, and I was determined to conquer this too.

The expensive, world-famous toxicologist I had been seeing told me he knew what was wrong with me, but he didn't know how to help me. I kept hearing your voice: "Pick yourself up by your bootstraps and keep going." So, that's what I did. I drove to the cliffs and watched the sun on the water or walked into the woods and sat under a tree, scribbling in my journal all the things I felt. If I unloaded emotional toxicity, maybe my body would have a better chance at recovery. I wrote forgiveness letters to everyone. I prayed for my enemies. I hated thinking I had enemies. What did I do to them? I went to cousin Joannie's pastor and had him pray with me to help me forgive the homeowners who had created this hellish situation with their hate.

I *had* to forgive to emotionally detox, but it wasn't easy. Emotional toxins are just as bad as environmental ones, and I knew enough about healing by this point in my life to take this emotional part seriously. I asked God to give me the strength to forgive. I knew anyone who could watch me go through such a disaster and look the other way had to have something missing inside them. I prayed for *their* healing.

I became sensitive to chemical smells. They were everywhere: restaurants, department stores, bookstores, coffee shops; I could smell toxic chemicals no matter where I went or what I did. I forced myself to do a daily swim. It's meditative value was healing. I put in my diamond studded earrings when I swam to remind myself there is beauty to be had, even in this dark time. Can you see it, Mom, diamonds and my bathing suit? You used to get upset when I wore bracelets with jeans. What would you think about this? I did what it took to keep my spirits high.

My journals were filled with prayers for recovery. I wrote to angels; I wrote to God. I wrote and wrote. I think writing kept me alive. I know writing kept me living in faith, hope, and empowerment. Writing was my way to make myself visible and matter, even though everyone I thought I knew well enough to trust betrayed me. My pen never betrayed me.

But hope was not completely lost, Mom. One day I had to go to the storage shed to clear out more of my toxic belongings and send them to the dump. I was heartbroken, as you can imagine, and still weak and feeling poisoned from the mold. I knew I would have to lift many heavy plastic cartons and I wondered how I would reach up to get some of them, because the movers stacked them quite high. I started praying prayers of gratitude and thankfulness. I repeated: "Thank you God for giving me the strength to do what I have to do." Why get angry at God? I needed him on my side.

I lifted one heavy container after the other, chanting loudly. I was exasperated, but I knew if I stopped chanting, I would fall apart. I couldn't give in to grief or anger, two emotions just as toxic as the situation I was in. I needed to rise out of this emotion.

If I got sicker, then what? Who was going to jump to my rescue and manage all that had to be done? I couldn't let myself give in or give up. A few minutes later, a red-hot convertible drove into the storage center and caught my attention. It was a fabulous car, but I had a lot to do, so I started lifting more containers.

Suddenly, I heard a man's voice call out: "Stop, stop, stop!"

I looked up to see my ex-neighbor Peter—six-foot-three muscle man Peter. He got out of his car and ran over to me. He wouldn't let me touch a thing. He moved all my cartons. God didn't send one of my weak, short friends or someone too busy to help. He sent Peter, the perfect person. How could you not realize that times like these had to come from a higher wisdom? How could you ever experience these events and not feel God's hand taking care of you?

I remember, Mom, when you spent months trying to save an organization I belonged to from financial ruin. You realized the woman running the organization was embezzling and you acted immediately to save all the work the teens had put into it. You started getting drawings of rats and hate mail. We almost lost the organization, but no one cared.

I remember the phone calls at night telling you ugly things. I admired your strength and resolve to do the right thing for the girls even though it was many of those same girls who shunned and hated you. How you kept doing what you knew was right taught me a lot. You never spoke ill of them or hated them back. You didn't try to defend or explain all you had risked keeping the organization alive. You took it on and paid no attention to them.

I thought of you a lot during my horrible dark years of being hated by an association I served for ten years. I heard people talk about me. I watched them shun me. I wanted so badly to talk to you. I needed advice on how to stay strong. I needed your willpower. I prayed and prayed and prayed and prayed. I hated feeling misunderstood, but I gave those people permission to think whatever they wanted and prayed again for the strength to give them forgiveness.

The situation was indefatigably miserable, and I wanted to rush to find a home, rush to get settled, rush to get well. I could hear your other aphorism: "Hurry up, hurry up." I thought that was the only way to survive suffering until I realized I had no place to hurry up to. But I'm not a Buddha. I was on a wild and nasty ride, and I didn't want to develop a philosophy about suffering—I wanted the suffering to stop! A terribly difficult lesson for someone like me who has little patience for suffering, or for anything for that matter. I never saw the point of any suffering before, but now I understood it was helping me build resilience. Without building resilience, I was on a path to a nervous breakdown.

The world had thrown me away. I was misjudged, criticized, mistreated, but I surprised myself with internal resources. Being Ruth's daughter and Jenny's great-granddaughter, Lily's granddaughter and Josefa's granddaughter, I knew one thing: I had what I needed somewhere tucked deep inside me. I knew God would never give me such a disabling experience and abandon me. It strengthened my faith, the faith I wondered about when I was eight, standing on the corner in the freezing weather.

My dear cat, Rainbow, was suffering as well. It broke my heart to see her suffering and traumatized, but I couldn't change my situation or hers. My friend Mike, who helped me with the mold, often left Santa Cruz to search for homes up and down the coast to remodel and sell.

I started to learn about the impact of suffering on mental health and the ways to keep myself stabilized as much as a homeless, ill, fifty-year-old could do. I learned how to get up from severe fatigue and move forward even just a half an inch at a time. This fatigue wasn't the same as after the near-death experience. Instead, it was from emotional distress, grief, anger, and insurmountable losses.

I bought a subscription to *Our Toxic Times,* because as meager as that bulletin was, it was the only publication that addressed the detailed concerns of someone trying to recover from mold. Dr. Vrana's website, "The Mold Source," was invaluable. And Dr. Vrana allowed me to call him whenever I needed information I couldn't get elsewhere. He was comforting and informative. Having someone with compassion and information to reach out to makes you never give up hope. He told me he started the website after he nearly died of black mold himself. One day his daughter walked in with a single piece of paper from their storage shed and he had a severe reaction to it. I understood. I too had similar reactions to things most people thought was simply neurotic. They had no idea how the body worked under such acute poisoning.

The Buddhists say when your dreams turn to dust, vacuum. Not my favorite household chore in the best of circumstances.

One more thing before I move on, Mom. I noticed through this soul-tearing experience that the more I suffered and discovered parts of myself, the more I thought of you, and the more our relationship began to change, to transform, to heal. There is something about suffering through your core that catalyzes an understanding for the suffering of others. I knew you were suffering greatly after Grandma died. I wish I had understood more about the mother/daughter bond back then. We could have talked and remembered Grandma together. I am certain that would have helped you, and it would have helped me. I didn't grieve her death until decades later when I realized I hadn't because grief was not something we ever spoke about. Now it seemed grief was about all I felt.

FIFTY-THREE

I bumped into my friend Charlie, whom I met in a healing class after my near-death experience in 1988. He was coming out of the gym and had recently become an acupuncturist. After listening to my health issues, he said he could help.

"I specialize in immune issues and allergies. Come see me!"

I enthusiastically took Charlie up on his offer. We worked together twice a week for thirteen months doing NAET treatments. Charlie listened to me and my body. He always asked me what foods I craved. I told him licorice and grapefruit. He laughed and told me those two things proved my adrenals needed support.

As we worked together, my body began to get stronger. It was a slow restoration, but I could feel it, despite the continued sensitivity and disturbing physical symptoms. I listed twenty-two symptoms from man-made chemicals, and Charlie told me to keep going, don't give up. My body had been seriously assaulted and this was not a quick fix.

I learned through my research that we are exposed to 80,000 chemicals a day. Can you imagine my distress? Trying to avoid them was crazy making. All this from the intense exposure to mold that could have and ought to have been avoided! The messy life I was left with brought down my faith in human beings and I struggled with this. If I couldn't count on others what kind of life was I looking at? I had to believe there were good people in the world. I focused on Charlie. He was good. Mike was good. Peter was good.

* * *

I searched the newspapers for a non-toxic home, the paper spread out over my steering wheel, the water glistening in the sun in front of me. I found one that seemed like a healthy option. It was a small room with hardwood floors, no carpet, not much of anything else. It had one tiny closet, a cabin-sized sink and small refrigerator, and no kitchen. It looked out into a large yard where the owner had planted an organic garden. I moved in. I had no furniture, no cleaning or other products, no closet full of clothes, nothing but a cotton yoga mat to sleep on, one set of pajamas, one old pair of jeans and an old black turtleneck, which I had on. I missed my comfortable life.

Santa Cruz had one small shop with organic clothing, and I realized organic (no pesticides or dyes) was all my symptoms could handle. Almost every day I walked out of the store with a small shopping bag of necessities and a receipt for at least $500. I was shocked at how expensive everything was. I never thought I would ever pay such prices for everyday necessities, but I had no choice. It was either that or continue to wear the same old pair of jeans that had started to shred and a faded black turtleneck. My few remaining friends laughed, oblivious to the seriousness of my health. They teased me that I was like Job in the Bible and said maybe I should live in a bubble. Many of them stopped paying attention or caring. It was a lonely journey.

For hope and strength, I read Maya Angelou's poem, "Still I Rise," and chanted it every morning as I pounded on the wooden floor with resolve that chemical corporations and poor legislation were not going to bring me down. I already survived a near-death experience, and I was steadfast in surviving this too.

Eventually, Charlie's acupuncture treatments enabled me to travel to other states to check out rural areas in search of a home. Friends gave me ideas—Paradise, California, Prescott Valley, Arizona. But traveling was exhausting, and it took a toll on me. I took flights, rented cars, learned how to drive around unknown cities, paid for B&Bs and hotel rooms saturated with perfume smells and cleaning products. I could have spun a globe and stopped it with my finger. I had no idea where to try next. I thought of New Mexico. I had taken writing workshops in Taos and thought I could move there. I liked Santa Fe.

Sitting in the sun in my landlord's organic garden, the water from her fishpond sending delicate water sounds into the air, I called a realtor in Santa Fe with a real estate magazine opened on my lap. I told the realtor who answered the reason for my search for a home and explained travelling was exhausting. If I made the trip out to Santa Fe, they would have to spend the entire time I was there taking me to see homes, because if we didn't find anything, I wouldn't go back. They had one shot to find a home my body could tolerate. I flew out and stayed in a motel converted from an adobe home in Santa Fe. I reacted to the smell of the sheets and called the office. The woman washed them several times, but the perfume wouldn't leave the fabric. She understood and told me she had many guests staying with her because they were in search of non-toxic living in Santa Fe. Not only did Santa Fe offer natural adobe homes, the high altitude also offered better air. I pushed through the night, grateful for her lack of criticism or frustration.

The realtor picked me up at the Guadalupe Inn at eight and dropped me off every night at five. He scheduled thirty-five houses to show me in three days. Each one left me with brain fog, a headache, or a mouth burning from formaldehyde. On the last day, as we drove away from the last home on his list, I wanted to cry. He looked across the road and asked, "Why didn't I see that one?"

It was a beautiful adobe home on five acres. He searched through his listing. It wasn't there because it was twice as expensive as my budget allowed but it was real adobe and seemed to meet most of my health criteria. He suggested we call the owner and see if we could view it while we were sitting outside. I couldn't afford it, but to save my life, what choice did I have? I decided to take a risk. The owner couldn't show it until morning. My hopes rose. The realtor looked relieved. If I could get well enough to work again, I would be able to make it work. I *had* to make it work. My choices were narrowing.

He picked me up the next morning, bright and early. The two-year-new adobe sat on five acres with many 200-year-old pinion and juniper trees around it. The realtor said I was brave to buy a place where I didn't know anyone, with no job and grave health concerns. Brave? I wasn't brave. I was a desperate woman trying to save her life. How much courage does it take to run for air when you can't breathe? No woman wants to be alone, sick, homeless, without an income. I was fifty-four. Scared? Yes. Determined? Yes. Brave? No.

In the short amount of time I walked through the rooms, my body had fewer reactions than any other house, so I decided to take a chance. It had almost thirty-five windows, and there seemed to be a nice breeze across the land. Perhaps I could open the windows and keep the air circulating until my body adjusted. I was willing to put myself in debt and hope opportunities arose.

I headed back to California to tie up loose ends and pack my few possessions, which fit nicely on the back seat of my Toyota Tercel. I gave notice to the landlord, thanked Charlie, and stepped into my future. I shared my trip plans with Mike, who gracefully agreed to drive ahead of me to New Mexico so he could make sure I got there safely. Thank you, God! My only question: Was I well enough to drive for three days?

The day came to leave California and move to New Mexico. I drove south out of Santa Cruz following Mike. Santa Cruz had become my home. Having moved there at twenty-two, I watched Santa Cruz grow from a small retirement town to a built-up busy city. Other than old bungalows and the new university, there wasn't much there in the 70s. The streets didn't even have streetlights on Pacific Garden Mall. The town shut down at three and on weekends.

Tears blurred my vision as I drove away from the beach town I had loved for thirty-three years. I fought the swell of hate for all those who took my accomplished life and stomped it in the mud.

I was leaving my beloved beaches, the hiking trails in the mountains, the sand dunes, the restaurants, the dense and fragrant smell of the redwood trees, the smell of salty ocean air, the full moon at night as it melted into the ocean's tiny ripples. I would miss the white freeway daisies, so cheery on foggy days, the coffee shops, the harvest moon rising over Capitola's beach in October, the warm winter days at the beaches, the bark of the harbor seals, the otters breaking clam shells on their chests as I ate breakfast on the wharf, the forest of Asilomar, the sand dunes at La Selva Beach. My losses felt insurmountable. I had to stop. I was breaking my own heart over and over. I focused on a highway of unfamiliar sights and Mike's white van in front of me. I had to keep driving into the unknown. I tried to ignite an excitement for a new chapter, but I hadn't quite let go of the old one yet. I couldn't look back. I couldn't say goodbye. Sometimes moving on seems monumental.

It had been four years since the mold began ravishing my life. I gripped my steering wheel. How many years would it take to recover? A screeching howl of pain erupted from deep inside my gut. I sounded like a wounded wolf. Grief, anger, sadness, fury, powerlessness erupted at once. I didn't doubt it anymore, Mom—people can be pure evil. But evil people will not make me become like them, which is what happens when you do to others as they have done to you. Studying philosophy taught me that I oversaw how I thought, not anyone else, and I was going to make sure it stayed that way. I caught myself in weak moments, but if I allowed myself to come back to forgiveness, I felt better about everyone, especially myself.

I stayed behind Mike's white van for three days, trying to envision the new chapter of hope and healing I was advancing into. Each exhausting hour of driving tested my fortitude. I wanted to pull over on the side of the road and curl up in a ball. I had to tell myself that despite my body's plea to rest, I was well enough to make this journey. I had to be, so I insisted I was and refused to listen to my failing energy. Much of the highway was under construction, like my life, and driving in the night required I remain sharply focused. I decided to chant something to keep my mind steady and thought of T.D. Jakes.

I heard him once say, "When God strips you down to nothing, He is up to something." Okay, God, just what are you up to? The days that followed were both the best of times and the worst of times, so let's take a breath together, order another sandwich, and I'll pick up my story again.

So now, Mom, I want to tell you about another vision I had a couple dozen times while I was living with my ex-boyfriend, one that was about to manifest. I stopped having them after I left him and never thought about them again. This wasn't the usual prophetic night dream; it was a day vision that flashed in front of me during waking hours. As quickly as it came, was as quickly as it disappeared. Shortly after I moved to New Mexico I remembered these visions.

I was in my thirties, which was my age at the time of these visions. I had a long braid draped down my back to my knees, which is how I wore my hair at the time of these visions. I wore a green layered skirt exactly like the one I made during the time of these visions. I wore brown strapped sandals, like the Nine West sandals I also wore during the time of these visions, and I walked around an adobe house on red dry dirt surrounded by small pinion trees. This natural environment was not where I was living at the time of these visions; I lived two blocks from the ocean.

My mood was melancholy, and as I walked slowly around the envisioned adobe home, I could feel the sun on my back. I walked thoughtfully, meditatively, as if the weight of the world were on my shoulders and I needed to find a solution to a life problem. It seemed strange that I never had the visions after I bought my townhouse and, in fact, I didn't even remember them. But the visions manifested more than two decades later.

I had no explanation for anything anymore. It was not as simple as figuring out what lesson could be learned and then moving on. I knew nothing about the desert or how to survive in it. I only knew that once I took that first step out of California with hopes of rebuilding in New Mexico, there was no way to turn back.

FIFTY-FIVE

Finally, in March 2005, Mike and I drove into Albuquerque, a delicate layer of snow falling over us as winter winds pushed against our cars. I followed Mike into a vista point to rest, then Mike drove away toward Santa Fe. When I turned the key in my ignition, it wouldn't start. I panicked. Would Mike notice I wasn't behind him? I turned the key again . . . nothing. I sat in my cold car wondering what to do. Thinking I might have flooded my car, I rested for a moment then tried again. Still my engine refused to start. It seemed it was as reluctant to enter this new life as I was. Mike soon returned and jump-started my car then away we drove down snowy streets, our wipers flapping. I was grateful I hadn't had to do this drive alone.

We finally drove into the town of Lamy, but I had no idea where my new home was. Mike waited as I searched my purse for my new address, but it wasn't there. I found the number for the realtor's office and Mike called them for directions. It seemed crazy I didn't have my new address in my purse, but I didn't. I was learning that being traumatized changed my ability to focus on details. We drove down a few driveways, but nothing looked familiar. Mike remained steady and calm, while I seemed to be floating somewhere. I couldn't get focused; the long drive had wiped out what little energy and concentration I had. Mike's sense of direction was enviable, and I trusted him. We drove back onto Hwy 95 and turned right on the next road. Within ten minutes I was following Mike down my long driveway. I took a breath. I was here. I arrived. I did it. We did it. I wanted to drop on the dirt and sob but, quite frankly, couldn't find the energy to do so. Now I had to get well, find a job, take care of this big, beautiful home, and get established in a new community. I had to make this huge move work. My financial resources were limited, and I couldn't do anymore moving and packing and running around looking for a safe place to breathe because I was beyond exhaustion.

I looked at Mike. His face was flushed, and he seemed on the verge of a panic attack. Here I was finally able to take a deep breath in the clean desert air, and Mike couldn't breathe. He said he thought he was experiencing altitude sickness and quickly unloaded my pole lamp, skis, and golf clubs from his truck, almost throwing them into my two-and-a-half-car garage. He quickly ran through the house to see it, and within sixty seconds I watched him speed down the driveway.

I stood there in tears, watching him leave. I didn't get to hug him goodbye or thank him for all he had done. I simply adored Mike. We had become good friends, and it was a gift to have a compassionate and helpful person in my life when I needed one most. He was my angel. Angels appear at just the right time, don't they, Mom?

So, there I was, my few possessions scattered on the concrete floor of my garage, keys in hand, and a stillness around me I had never breathed into before. My realtors showed up with a pizza, Santa Fe style, which meant it was topped with hot chilis. It was spicy, but delicious. After they left, I looked around my big empty house. I stared out the large glass windows into space, so much space, the mountains in the far background encircling my home. I had no idea how to live in the desert, but I had embarked upon a new adventure, and I was soon going to find out.

I moved my few containers into my spacious empty bedroom, then walked the five acres to get acquainted with my new environment.

In the near distance I studied the Sangre de Cristo, Ortiz, and Santa Fe Mountains. Their strength surrounded me on all sides. I took a deep breath, the cold air biting my lungs. The air was welcoming, clean, soothing, empowering. For the first time in years, I was able to breathe without the sting of chemicals raking my lungs.

There were fifteen 200-year-old pinion and juniper trees, several kinds of cacti, yucca plants, and other foliage I couldn't identify. I examined a tall cactus and noticed a bright pink flower blossom just beginning to open. The color was exquisite and fully captured my attention. I must have stood there for three full minutes, just staring into its glory. My eyes filled with tears. Colors were definitely more stunning in the desert. I studied every plant and tree on the land.

I looked around. Not a soul in sight. I wanted to share this experience, but for now I just held it close to my heart. What a gift to have been led to this place of all the places I could have wound up. God knew just what I needed for healing: the power of mother nature. It was difficult to believe this was my home, so beautiful, so spacious, such fresh air. And again, I can't say this strongly enough, I could breathe for the first time in years without my tongue stinging, my nose and lungs burning, or my brain being submerged in deep fog.

SURPRISES

jaded by life's challenges
I escaped to the desert
and found a foreign world

that startled me back to life

cacti blossoms radiantly showed off hot pink blossoms
yucca plants stood erect their waxy white bells bowing
Mexican hat wildflowers red and yellow intertwined
with buffalo grass

drunken crickets the color of granny smith apples
walked sideways
miniature ancient pinion trees dotted the land
purple sage plants spread wide
mountains changed colors at dusk

ant hills mounded in raised piles
spiders varied in stripes, spots, and hues the size of
golf balls as long as a stick of chewing gum

snakes dressed in geometric patterns some
red, thin as a pencil fast as a train
some wearing skins of green lazily slithered for a day's
walk
road runners dragged their long tails barely touching
ground

quail led a trail of teeny babies showing off new families
bunnies born from shallow holes cautiously climbed to
ground
jack rabbits the size of dogs leapt across the land

horny toad lizards walked into the sun out of mud huts
others canary yellow and baby blue raced under bushes

bumble bees the size of chicken eggs fed on lobelia

bushes
coyotes sang in the dark to those miles away

moths like sage green lace decorated walls in the sun
or were dark grey as big as shoes with one large orange
dot on pure white under wings

tumbleweeds sped with alacrity as if being chased by
demons
winds whipped adobe walls howling

triple rainbows followed vibrant storms wide and
hopeful
iridescent ravens cleaned up dead things
sky at dusk brilliant in purple, orange, yellow, pink,
green, and blue welcomed the night

silent whisperings of God omnipresent to those who
listened
space

lots of space

Let me tell you about my new home, Mom. You would have loved it. It was a two-year-old real adobe designed in the old adobe style, which means every room opened onto a large courtyard. My bedroom had a second courtyard on the other side of the large courtyard, and in the corner was an adobe kiva. The large courtyard had its own kiva, as did my living room. The living room, dining area, and kitchen opened into one large rectangular room. Down the hallway were two bedrooms, a bathroom, pantry, and closet. All closets were walk-ins with lights. Off this hallway was a room with a sink, washer, and dryer. This was the entrance to the large garage. The entire home was sectioned into three heating elements. They were heated with radiant heat, which meant heat came up from the floors, warming the floors first, not the air. My bedroom had a separate room attached to it for an office or nursery, a large walk-in closet and a bathroom with a bear claw tub, large windows, a separate room for the toilet with a large window, and a large shower with two shower heads.

This was my dream house. If I were to have a home to make up for the distress and trauma of the last five years, this was it. I only hoped I'd be able to make enough money to keep it, but I couldn't think about that. I simply had to get well enough to find work. I had to find a holistic doctor that understood mold and chemical sensitivity, a dentist, a hairdresser. I needed to start all over again with everything. And I needed to rest. I so very badly needed to rest.

After I got as oriented as I could in a few short hours, I took a shower and headed for the living room. I sat on the slate floor (of course, I had no furniture) and turned on the ceiling lights nailed into gorgeous pine vigas, which ran across the ceiling through the entire 2300-square-foot home. There were no lights on the roads in the desert, so it was pitch black outside. The homes were acres apart from each other, and I could barely see the other homes around me.

As I tried to read to the dim lights on my ceiling, not noticing they had dimmer switches and were on low, I noticed out of the corner of my eye a foot-long centipede, blue, purple, and clear, racing against the corner of the wall. Luckily, I had a broom and ran for it in my bare feet across the long room to the pantry. I reached it before it slid into what was going to become my writing room and quickly swept the long critter a foot at a time across the slate floor until I got to the large glass front doors. I quickly opened them and with a heavy swipe, swept the centipede out into the desert blackness. I immediately shut the doors because I had no idea what might be out there, and I didn't want anything running, slithering, or creeping in.

So much for my shower; I was soaked with sweat from the rush of the event. I braced myself for many unknowns. I realized the desert does not belong to humans; the city belongs to humans. The desert belongs to mother nature and is sacred ground. The land wasn't pruned by gardeners. It was unadulterated, raw, alive all on its own accord. It told you who it was. I can say this, Mom, I fell in love with it as foreign as it all was on that first day. More deeply, I sensed that every preconception I had about life or spirituality, or healing was going to be awakened here.

In the morning, I needed to find a grocery store, but my car engine wouldn't turn over. I plugged in my phone to call AAA and despite the insistent promises of the phone company that my service would be up and running, the line was dead. With environmental illness, the EMF from cell phones is a nightmare, but having no other choice, I flipped open my cell phone and made a call to AAA.

The man who arrived at my door said there was a mechanic shop two miles down the road and not to worry. He dropped me and my car off and left.

I stood on the New Mexico red dirt lapping up the warm sun on a chilly March day. The mechanic examined my car and said he needed to keep it overnight. I explained I had no one to pick me up and, worse, I had no idea how to get back home. I was still in a blur and hadn't paid attention to how AAA got to the mechanic's shop. I hadn't expected they would need my car overnight. I asked the mechanic if he could drive me home after he finished for the day. He was not happy with my request. I would wait all day in the winter sun if I had to. This I could do. This was a mild obstacle compared to the challenges of the last five years. While I was speaking with the mechanic, trying not to sound desperate, a customer standing nearby overheard my conversation. She seemed to have compassion for my plight, offered to drive me home, put my address in her GPS, and off we went.

I commented I had just arrived yesterday and had no food, but I could fast for a day until I got my car back. After what I had just come through these challenges were merely a blip in the day. They had no distressful power over me. The woman reached into her trunk and brought out two bags of groceries. She said she had just come from Wild Oats. I had no idea what Wild Oats was, but I was grateful. Was she sure she wanted to give me all her food? Could I pay her? Could I cook for her? She shook her head and said all was good, she was happy to help me. She came in to quickly see my home giving me an opportunity to share my amazing new abode, then left. Angels, Mom. I seemed to be surrounded by angels.

After I enjoyed some of the prepared salads, I walked on my land to explore my five acres. Two tiny bunnies had just been born under trash the previous owners left against a wall. I saw a jackrabbit take large jumps across my land, appearing at first to be a large dog. His ears gave him away, and I couldn't help but laugh at his ridiculously looking self. Later I saw a large black and white bull snake, which didn't drive me wild from its beauty, not at first. In the middle of my driveway, I spotted a canary yellow and baby blue lizard that took my breath away. A colorful spider long and thick, had spun a huge web in the corner of two of my walls. It was speckled with snow drops and looked like a pearl and diamond necklace. I lost count of the many plants, moths, and birds I saw for which I had no names. I was living in a Walt Disney movie. I wanted to scream my excitement into the air. This wasn't just a new home; this was a magical environment. I had no idea the desert was so rich with life. I wanted to know more, how to take care of every living thing, how to manage, and I felt an awesome responsibility to do so. I vowed to kill nothing I didn't absolutely have to.

The next morning as I started to brush my teeth in my new beautiful bathroom, I felt a tickle on my ankle. I looked down to see a black beetle delicately trying to get traction to walk up my leg. I called down to it, "is your tickle welcoming me?" It stopped and looked up at me. I swear it was listening to me. I scooped it up, placed it outside and watched it eagerly move into the ground cover. Later I found out the beetle was a stink bug. It was on the list of endangered species. They usually lift their butts when feeling threatened, emitting a horrible stink, but this one didn't do that. I was grateful. I heard their smell is quite repulsive.

As I was setting up my computer in my new writing room, a radiant black and yellow bird landed on a branch leaning up against my window. I had never seen a bird so starkly beautiful. This is what I needed: fresh air and the presence of unadulterated beauty. Everywhere I looked I saw nature in its most innocent and vibrant form. With each step onto my land, I found something new. I found hope being restored and my joy for life returning.

Not one week into my new life, while standing at the stove scrambling eggs, a sharp pain shot up over my right ear. It nearly brought me to my knees. It was like the pain that hit me after you died while my boyfriend and I were on a sky lift. I thought I was going to fall to the ground. Perhaps it was the same situation— calming down after a crisis. I wasn't sure. All I can say, Mom, was that it was unnerving, and I couldn't move. I became overwhelmed with the thought of having to find a doctor so soon after my move. There were so many things to do first to get my life in order.

On the slate ledge around the kiva was my six-inch-by-six-inch black and white TV I got free from a local department store in Santa Cruz after spending a certain amount of money on Christmas gifts. The only channel I got reception for was dedicated to ministry. I had found ministry shows soothing and watched them each morning when I had the opportunity. Friends I had counted on had become quite judgmental of my hard times but the ministers on those shows gave me reassurance and educational sermons on ways to spiritually deal with hard times. And I was still in hard times. These powerful sermons saved me from further distress. Those hours became my sacred time to enter into prayer.

As I walked with my plate of eggs to the living room still vacant of any furniture, I sat on the floor to get some spiritual food for the day. The woman praying for her audience declared, "There is someone in the audience who has pains in her head shooting up over her right ear. The pains are frightening her and she is unnerved by it. This woman is considering seeing a doctor."

I stopped chewing. Was she talking about me? The woman and her male prayer partner held hands and prayed for the audience member to be healed. Suddenly, the pain above my ear stopped. It didn't return for the rest of the day nor the next. I wrote them a testimonial. I wished I could have called you, thank you for letting me know God was real. Now I was seeing it on my own. I don't believe things happen randomly; everything has a purpose. Even the last five years, with their unwanted and traumatic changes, had happened for a reason. I had no idea what that reason was yet, and maybe I wouldn't know for decades to come. But I knew one day I would look back and be able to make sense of it.

A few days later, I awoke early to a fiery orange light pushing through my bedroom window. I thought my land was on fire and panicked. Running barefoot across the flagstone and pea pebble walkway in my courtyard, I flung open the door and nearly dropped to the ground. Before me was the most radiant orange sunrise. Sounds hyperbolic, Mom, but I assure you it isn't. I spent most of my weekends in California in nature. I was either at the beach or hiking in the woods. At night I enjoyed watching the moon on the water. But the natural environment in New Mexico was something else.

Remember Norman? We have kept in touch through letter writing for decades. You remember how I loved having a pen pal when I was a young girl? Today, in my seventies, Norman and I have been pen pals for decades. Anyway, he wrote and asked me why I liked living in the desert; he just couldn't imagine me living in dirt. I had to laugh and wrote him back a long letter explaining how beautiful the desert was, even the red dirt!

Oh, and Sharon, remember her from Brooklyn, Mom? Sharon was a lifeline while I was transitioning my life from California to New Mexico. She called me every two to three months to check in on me. Her calls were an act of true friendship. Listening to someone venting about trauma even if mixed with a new wonderful experience, isn't easy. I had a deep need to talk about what I was living through and the difficulties I was still facing. I spoke far too long at times, but Sharon simply let me vent my distress. I could hear her walk away from the phone to do other things, but she was patient and kind. She didn't interrupt my venting with how busy she was or that she was tired of listening to me. She still responded to me even if she had walked into another room. Sometimes I felt guilty because I took a lot of her time, but I had to speak about my trauma and transition experience. Hearing my story helped me process it. She never complained or stopped calling. She was there in the way I needed a friend, and I was and still am deeply grateful.

Winter was still happening in early April and one morning I awoke to several feet of newly laid snow. Remember those Christmas cards with snow covered in glitter that always ended up everywhere? That's what the land looked like. Luckily, I had just purchased a shovel, so I got as warmly dressed as I could manage with my few pieces of clothing and headed out to shovel. I had forgotten how strenuous shoveling was those days I used to help dad during our Brooklyn winters. Before I was one-third down my long driveway, I'd be down to a thin shirt sweating profusely.

As the weather began to warm up, the circle of pinion and juniper trees at the end of my property had become a favorite place to meditate. One early morning I awoke with a heavy sense that one of the pinion trees was calling me. I quickly donned my old pair of jeans, put on my hiking boots, and ran out to see what the problem was.

I wish I could have called you to tell you about this. Around one of the pinions was an entangled pile of tumbleweed. I got a sense the tree was suffocating, and even more strangely, I felt like I was suffocating too. I ran back to the house to get some work gloves I had recently bought, then got on my knees and started pulling and tugging at the tumbleweed. It was not an easy task; they are nasty bushes. I don't know how long I spent extricating them from around the tree, but when I finally got the tree free of the tumbleweed I swear, Mom, I heard the tree take a deep sigh, as did I.

* * *

My hope that my new home would be without disastrous smells was short-lived. Within two weeks I began reacting to the smell of formaldehyde but had no idea where it was coming from. Wasn't my adobe home, *real* adobe? I opened the phone book and dropped my finger on a contractor's name, then called the number. The contractor called me soon after, said his secretary heard the desperateness in my voice and told him he had to call me right away. He showed up ready to work at five o'clock, after he had finished a full day at his construction site. He said he was glad I contacted him because clients were calling him to remove products he had just installed because they were getting sick from them. He was so kind and sweet. His name was James, and together we got busy learning about how my real adobe home was built and how to remediate it to get rid of the formaldehyde smells.

I brought out a brochure for a product I began using in California. He called the company and got an understanding of what issues might be causing my distress. We ordered some of their products, then got to work. I couldn't believe I was up to my eyebrows in more house issues. But this time I had a wonderful contractor and good person helping me.

Exposed plywood on unfinished tops of cabinets, toxic insulation installed around pipes inside the walls, and plywood used in rooms that were not adobe were the culprits.

Every night for three months James showed up at my house after work and often on weekends. We ripped up the carpet and laid tile. I had to trust my money would not run out and I would soon be healthy enough to find work and start replenishing my fast-dwindling savings. I was living on God's mercy and grace.

I must stop here, Mom, to remind you of that vision from the 80s, the one in which I was walking on red earth around an adobe home surrounded by trees. I was now living this vision. Strange but true.

James was working in the kitchen when I stepped outside. As I bent over and touched the earth in the warm sun to pray for healing, Nana's energy instantly settled by my right shoulder. It was strong and alive. I raced into the house to get my pen to write down the experience, startling James. He asked me what the rush was. I called out, "I must write this down," then sat at my desk and wrote about Nana's appearance when I began to pray. Her presence became alive in the desert. Maybe New Mexico brought me closer to my Latino roots; she was with me all the time.

Sometimes I would see Dad sitting in the corner of my bedroom, crying. It was more than distressing. Maybe he knew what the people I was about to meet would do to me. Had I not met a single human there my life might have remained easier, but because I like having a lot of friends, I set out making them. I quickly learned some more hard lessons about people. And I had to face lessons to learn about myself as well. I remained open to gleaning whatever I could out of the time I was in Lamy. I suspected this experience was simply another temporary step I had to take.

A few days after Nana's presence, a hummingbird appeared outside my bedroom window as I was making my bed. It appeared eye-level as if it were watching me. Then, as hummingbirds do, it flitted away. Later it stared at me through my living room window as I washed the floors. This occurrence happened several times in a week, and although I found it interesting, I didn't think too much of it until I went to the Frank Howard Gallery in Santa Fe with a writing friend who visited Santa Fe on vacation. In the gallery I turned a corner and stood staring into a large painting of an Indian woman with closed eyes, hummingbirds splayed around her. Goosebumps ran down my arms. The salesclerk told me hummingbirds meant a relative was returning to earth to spend time with you. How's that for odd, Mom? And I tell you, the hummingbird had Nana's essence.

* * *

My body started to calm, but I was still quite ill. I began a search for holistic doctors and practitioners. I found Dr. Laurent

Bannock; a clinical nutritionist educated in the UK and began working with him. I drove to Albuquerque for herbal treatments, which, according to Dr. Bannock's assessment while studying my cells under his microscope, helped my cells change their shape from jellybeans to healthy round circles. He showed me slides before and after my treatments. Still, I was quite reactive to chemical smells, so I did acupuncture. Everything helped a little, but the damage to my body was severe and was not going to change overnight. I had to keep going. I vacillated from deep distress to hope and everywhere in between.

Dr. Bannock sent me to the hospital for a series of blood tests, then reran those same samples through his own testing devices. He called me into his office to go over the results.

"According to the hospital tests, you are not sick."

I looked at him in utter distress because I knew I was.

"But," he said, "according to my more specific tests, you are right. You are sick."

I asked him if I had continued with my plans to have intravenous treatments in Carmel Valley, would I have gotten well by now. I had paid thousands to prepare for the treatments, but something told me those treatments weren't right, and I bolted from the office as soon as my name was called. Afterward, I drove home for three hours, condemning myself for not having gone through with the expensive treatment. Did I sabotage my wellness?

Dr. Bannock said it was a good thing I had left and didn't go through with the intravenous treatment. He said I would have died in the doctor's office, that I was far too sick and my body far too toxic to sustain an intravenous approach. He said that by listening to my inner voice, I did the right thing and saved my life.

Interesting life I'm living, huh? Are you ready to hear more, Mom? Maybe we should order another grilled cheese sandwich.

* * *

I set out down the road one chilly morning to get my mail. I loved walking directly on the desert earth instead of concrete. The Santa Fe Mountains were to my right and as the sun moved across the sky, I watched the colors hovering over them change. Caught by this shifting of colors, I heard a message deep inside me that despite my doubts of having moved out of California, I belonged right where I was. And I belonged to this wondrous universe. I had never felt a communion of belonging to the planet before. Something in me shifted and I noticed I was healing. I continued down the road comforted by the desert's quietness. It holds the voice of God. I wished you had been there too to feel better about yourself, to help you find peace. I was in conversation with nature all around me every day. I'd just be real still and listen. I swear, Mom, it was the world of God saying over and over, "You are home. We give you peace. You belong to us."

I didn't have the ache for my California life as much anymore. Sure, I missed the ocean and the Santa Cruz Mountains and the life I built there, but this world took me in, embraced me, and comforted me.

* * *

I met a young woman who had been over-exposed to black mold as I had. She had been an attorney and sculptor, but now she was disabled and couldn't work or sculpt. Her heart had taken the brunt of the mold poisoning, and she was on oxygen. She invited me to join a group of women who were all trying to recover from black mold. I felt lucky to have been invited into a support group so soon upon my arrival in New Mexico. We all sat in the sun in the courtyard of an adobe home sipping on tea. I expected we would share healing remedies and doctors and resources for a clean, chemical-free lifestyle. But five minutes into the discussion I realized all they wanted to do was sit and complain about how impossible it was to survive in such a toxic America. I felt sicker the longer they complained. Finally, I stood up and told them complaining wasn't on my agenda, and if they were only meeting to complain, I was going home. They looked at me stunned. I told them I thought our time would be better spent sharing our experiences, what things worked and didn't work, so we could get well. They were not interested in changing their attitude or their point of view on the group discussions, so I left.

The next day one of the women called and said they all liked me and wanted me to return. I told them I wouldn't. After I got home, I had been sick all night, trying to rid myself of their negative energy. I had made a hot bath and sat in it until the water turned cold. Their group took too much out of me. I wasn't going back unless they changed the conversation and purpose of the group. I had to focus on getting well and I knew getting well meant watching my thoughts with keen attention. I had to draw up my faith and I couldn't do that with a negative mindset. I couldn't re-design a life resenting all my losses or begrudging the loss of the comforts I once had. To move forward was requiring I let go of complaining about things I could not change.

* * *

As I met people in New Mexico they assumed I was retired, like most of my neighbors. They viewed me as a rich woman and envied my new home filling with new belongings. They began stealing from me as I bought things to rebuild a home. Even a few friends from California or other states saw me that way and they should have known better. They heard what I had been through. Then the country's economy was spiraling down, and those around me thought I wasn't affected by it. But I was on basic survival too. And I had lost so much of my savings I still had to work and still couldn't secure work. I don't believe anymore that people are going to be decent until they are.

I also learned nature can be cruel and I can't stop it. I learned I don't have to fix everything. The desert teaches you that life is precious, that includes mine.

One day I was writing at my desk and something out the window caught my eye. A bunny was jumping in playful hops, then a young snake raised its head. What was I watching? Could it be I was witnessing a baby snake in playful banter with a baby bunny?

I loved writing in the desert, in that deep stillness, hearing the susurrations in the wind. When I wasn't sitting somewhere on the land, I'd write inside the circle of pinion and juniper trees at the back of my property.

There were three apple trees along the wall of my garage, and although I don't like raw apples, I ate them as I worked on the land. Apples right off the branches are not like apples from a grocery store. These were surprisingly delicious. I wasted not one of them. In the spring, a wide circle of Mexican Hat wildflowers, along with other flowers I never found names for, mingled in with the buffalo grasses. The swath of browns, reds and yellows were striking. Tiny purple flowers climbed up one of the pinion trees. Yucca plants set up shoots of many white buds.

At night the sky was filled with constellations. Oh, Mom, you would have loved it. Without streetlights the sky has no interruptions. It can display all it has. During lightning storms, I'd move a chair up to one of my windows and watch lightning streaks of pink, yellow, white, blue, and green dance along the mountain tops. On the nights of a full moon, it seemed everything quieted to listen to it. If I could, I'd live in the desert forever. There was not one tiny speck of the desert that wasn't an example of our rich and magnificent planet. If only everyone could experience it. We'd love more.

Sunsets were vibrant with swirls of deep purple, yellow, orange, green, blue. The sky was an artist's palette. I loved the dense smell of hay from neighboring ranches after rain, and the triple rainbows that stretched for miles, so clear you could mark the borders of the colors.

Everything spoke to me. I was in constant dialogue with my environment. My attention was heightened. I breathed with the trees, the tumbleweeds, the red racer snakes slithering near my sage plants, mice trying to raise babies in the kiva, colorful moths spreading their wings on the sunbaked adobe walls.

No one could be bored in the desert. I think it would have taken you out of your anger and depression, and we could have explored this majestic part of the world together. I ached to share it with you.

The longer I lived in Lamy the longer I wanted to live in Lamy, but I knew deep within myself that my time there was going to be short-lived, not just because I couldn't find work and my savings was quickly dwindling, but because I had an internal knowing that this was simply a stop along the way.

Then, just as I came to this realization, I began to have visions again. Oh, Mom, this vision was disturbing. I was standing on a city street. Concrete streets and roads were everywhere, and in front of me was a mess of highways up in the air going in all directions. To my left were high telephone poles with many cables. It was so opposite the environment I was in now, I cringed and hoped it was not going to be my next move.

I had hoped this house and land would have become my permanent home. I needed to believe I would be able to build a place to rest and create and heal.

As a daughter of every strong and wise women in my family

line, I carry their language of strength and wisdom into all I have created, survived, and still hope for. You were my first teacher of creation. I suppose daughters learn what is to be learned from their mothers then go backwards through the generations, to their ancestors to learn more deeply who they are from. I am fortunate to have known the women in my family as far back as great grandma and both my grandmothers.

If only we could have sat in that circle of old trees and talked and healed. Maybe we could have brought all the women in our family into that circle too.

FIFTY-SIX

Despite twenty-plus years of social work experience, I could not find a full-time job, only short-term contracted work. Ageism is real, and I was fifty-six with a chronic illness.

I often reflected upon all the situations you went through, all the aphorisms you said whether I believed them or not, and the actions I watched you take. Sometimes I think, if mothers only knew how their daughters are constantly being challenged to become whole women, they might ally with their daughters more. Since all mothers are daughters, every woman knows the struggles and challenges of becoming whole.

Needing money, I no longer had the luxury to wait for what I wanted. So, I decided to pick up a forgotten dream and open a clothing store. But I was still reactive to chemicals in fabrics and had to find organic clothing. I began researching about organic clothing, where I could buy what I needed, and how to start a shop. The knowledge I gained from how our clothes and products are made prompted me to search for American companies with organic cotton farms. I found five including one that supported fair trade if they used their workforce from other countries.

I rented a 400-square-foot room in a strip mall on the plaza. It was expensive, but it was in the center of town. Tourists came in for both vacations and conferences, so I felt hopeful I'd have enough customers. I didn't realize, as a new resident, nor was I told by the landlord, that the main conference buildings were under construction and the tourist population had been greatly reduced. In addition, the country was in a downward economic spiral.

But desperate means calls for desperate measures. I had to do something to bring in money and this felt like my best idea outside of social work. I named my store JanetRuth's, my first name and our mutual middle name, so we could share this shop together. I even made the labels for the clothing with our baby photos next to each other. The labels were adorable. You always wanted to have your own store so, here it was—our store.

I knew retail therapy helped women feel better, but now I had the chance to see it up close and personal. I had one customer who was looking through a stack of cotton tops. She looked up at me and asked if I had ever been through a divorce, then broke out crying. For the next three days after her conference, she came in to seek a new look and overcome her heartache. Another woman tried on most of the clothes and looked great in almost all of them. But her husband stood at the door as she exited the dressing room and, without saying anything to her, made it known by his facial expressions which top he wanted her to buy—the one that sucked the color out of her face. I could feel her hesitation to please herself and her anxiety about displeasing him.

I purchased a bench for customers and waiting husbands who loved having me listen to their stories, because who doesn't enjoy being listened to? It was fascinating to me to watch a relationship with customers build over a few days just because I was listening to them while they shopped for clothes. Many commented that JanetRuth's was their favorite boutique in Santa Fe. I planned on buying a map of the world and letting customers stick pushpins in the places where they lived, but by that time I knew I had to close my shop. Maybe another time in another place.

The shop had been a lot of work. I bought, paid for, unpacked clothes, put them on shelves, priced them, and took all sales, then rebought inventory. I didn't mind it. JanetRuth's was a lot of fun. In addition to teaching my customers about the benefits of organic chemical-free clothing, I had the opportunity to share my wisdom about health, chemicals, healing, and so much more. And I listened for hours to customers' amazing healing stories of their own. Some had gotten quite ill but found ways to heal themselves after giving up on the medical profession. I started writing down their stories to put them together for a book. I crocheted organic cotton shawls and sold my own work as well. I hoped to find organic fabric and make my own clothing, but reality hit hard. The country was economically in a tailspin and my financial situation was doing the same.

In many ways starting my life anew felt as if I were trying to climb the stairs in a spook house, the landing so close yet so far. Financially, I was barely keeping my life pinned together. Many of my friends who visited from other states saw my new, beautiful Adobe home, visited my shop, and made inaccurate and disturbing assumptions. They saw what they wanted to see, despite any background I gave them about how I wound up in Lamy and opened a clothing store. Nothing about my home showed the trauma I had just lived through, nor the striving to overcome the trauma I was still experiencing. What is the measurement for knowing good people?

Naively, I wanted people to be happy for me. Instead, jealousy was weaponized against me stealing my things. I confronted those who stole from my home, but rarely did they admit it as if I didn't know my products and possessions were missing.

I reminded myself of something I read on the wall in one of my Santa Cruz offices:

I shall allow no man to belittle my soul enough to make me hate him.
— George Washington Carver

The list of those I wanted to forgive was getting longer, yet still I did not want to carry any sore feelings into my healing life. I decided to refuse to let the outside world tear me apart again. Truly, Mom, what could I do? It seemed the more determined I was to make peace, the more I was confronted with non-peaceful situations. I took a breath and added them to my forgiveness list I burned in my Kiva most nights as a cleansing ritual.

I kept mindful of those insistent words I heard back in my remodeled California kitchen:

There's always more!
There's always more!

There's always more possessions. There's always more people, more friends, more money, more houses. This is a rich and abundant universe. I learned from living on the land, watching the rhythms of nature, and listening to the wind that everything regenerates one way or another.

It took biting grit at times to rebuke anger towards them over their behavior towards me. And then I had an enlightening thought. I realized I was under no obligation to struggle to make the relationships become what I wanted them to be. I realized that I didn't have to invest in these friendships anymore and most importantly, I began to see that all I had to do was let them go. Why had I still resisted the letting go part? In pondering this question, I hit upon a deep vulnerable part of myself. I loved people. I wanted people to love me in return.

Sometimes it seems my days in the desert were biblical. That is, I was sent to the desert for great healing, to build faith and fortitude and a belief that everything happens for a reason and that I would always be provided for; perhaps also to turn my life over to God, because thinking I could take control and make it work my way was pure ignorance.

FIFTY-NINE

It is now 2009.

As I sat inside the circle of trees at the end of my property, a surreal force of energy started presenting me with impressions of a white man in his thirties. I saw him in a vision, quick and sharp. He wore a black apron. I thought he was trying to tell me something. It was strange, and I didn't pay any attention to it. A while later I met a shaman who asked me where I lived, and I mentioned the strong energy on my land. I shared with him the vision of the man wearing a black apron. He told me the man was a welder and that there were spirits waiting for me to sit inside the circle of trees to write their stories. I freaked. Was he telling me there were spirits who wanted to channel their stories through my pen?

I thought about these "spirits" for two years but couldn't bring myself to fulfill the request. I had read many books over the years that were channeled, but I never thought it would come around to me.

Financially, I had no choice but to put my home on the market. After I reluctantly did so, I knew if I didn't write the stories soon, it would be too late. So, one day I took my chair, tea, pen, and journal and sat in the circle of trees to see what would happen. At first nothing. As I was about to walk back to my house, I felt a pull at the back of my neck pushing me to sit and write. In eleven days, I wrote a dozen or more stories. I won't go into it all now, but it was the strangest book I have ever written. I titled the book *Voices from the Land*. What else would I call a book like that? Those voices were not the same inner voices or visions I had within myself over the years. Those voices weren't mine.

You are probably wondering how your daughter turned out to be so weird. I have no response for that.

* * *

The vision of the city of concrete and up-in-the-air highways started occurring regularly. Each time it appeared I cringed and tried to destroy, deny, and rebuke it. It was an awful scene. I hoped I was not headed there and couldn't imagine where such an ugly place existed.

Meanwhile I continued to look for work and was about to turn sixty. Sixty! There was no movement in any of the directions I had hoped for. Life seemed to be stagnating, and I was again stuck in instability with people, money, and health. Matters got so desperate the only food I had to eat was a pack of frozen peas. How could my life have fallen into such a bare place *again*? Wasn't New Mexico my place of healing, restoration, and moving on to the success I knew I could create? What was God up to now? All I could do was shudder in fear that more devastation was looming before me. I felt another riptide catching me in its grips and there wasn't a darn thing I could do about it.

I found myself praying to God—well, more like pleading, begging. "Please God," I cried out, "what do you want from me now?" I recalled that a shaman told me I had an angel who was guarding my front door to keep me safe. I told him I had a vision in which a large Indian walked past my front door as if on watch duty. I felt absolutely ridiculous admitting such a thing, but it was true. Over the years I lived in Lamy I heard many accounts from people with similar visions. In fact, almost all of them found trinkets on their property to support their visions. I, however, found no such things. The shaman simply nodded. People who lived in the desert had all sorts of surreal and crazy stories.

Back to having no food on my sixtieth birthday. As I opened the bag of frozen peas and began putting them in piles to see how many meals I could make from them, my neighbor Ann knocked on my front door. She asked what I was doing. I told her I had to close my shop, was still out of work, and was having a difficult time selling my beautiful home. I fought back tears and reassured her not to worry, because she was that kind of friend and neighbor, and I would find a way. I reminded myself of all I had survived. This seemed no huge deal in comparison. I could go on a fast. I could do something . . . couldn't I?

About an hour later a white van came up my driveway. It was Ann and her husband John. They came to my back door carrying seven plastic bags of food. I started crying. I had enough food for at least a month. I remembered God's message: "I will not forget you nor forsake you."

My time in the desert was the best of times and the worst of times. Each day was adventurous, and I much preferred the challenges of the desert to the destruction, greed, and evil I saw in some of the people I met there. For such a spiritual environment, you'd think there would be more sensitive people.

Then good fortune seemed to appear.

SIXTY-ONE

I got a call from a man who found my resume online. He hired social workers to work as civilians with military families stationed in Europe. Military life was hard on families, especially the kids. Because of my long history of working with teens and their family dysfunctions, I was offered a job. I spent the next six months complying with the government's demands for several interviews, three-hour clinical tests, and redesigning my resume to military style. I went to Montana for an intensive interview and to take computer competency tests. Everything seemed to be going in the right direction. I figured I would work in Europe until retirement, then I would retire in Costa Rica where life was more affordable. That was my plan. I was thrilled. It seemed positive changes were in the air.

I found a buyer for my home at the eleventh hour. I rented a condo for three weeks, waiting to leave for the job in Europe. One week before I was to surrender the rented condo to go back to Montana for further training, I received a call. The interviewer said he was pulling the job because of my chemical sensitivities. I assured him I would be fine, but he said he was cancelling the job just the same. I informed him I had just been on a military base in Europe for a week visiting my nephew's wife and had no problems (yes, Mom, you have a handsome grandson). But he was insistent. Why didn't he decide this before I spent six months complying with his distressing and exhausting requests? Turns out someone at one of the contracted jobs I had for three months wanted revenge after my supervisor hired me instead of her best friend. I was told this woman had decided to punish me for my supervisor's decision and played up my chemical sensitivity. I asked my supervisor why she didn't defend me, and she said she couldn't or she would have lost her job.

You must know, Mom, that I'm telling you the truth. I'm creative but I couldn't have made up some of these life experiences if I sat all day at the computer.

Having nowhere to go because my home was sold, I remained in the condo while I replanned my next move. That winter, Santa Fe had a hard freeze, and as I was making beef soup in the kitchen, I heard a series of loud pops. I watched water quickly run through the walls and over my feet. The pipes in the condo next to the one I was renting burst. I called James, my contractor. He arrived on the scene within minutes and shook his head in disbelief that again I was dealing with water problems. Although this time the property was not mine, I called the owner and prepared to move to a hotel.

In talking to a friend about where to go from here, she said she liked Austin because of the music. I contacted Amtrak and bought a one-way ticket to Austin. I called Austin's Chamber of Commerce, got the name of a realtor who helped new residents find a place to live, then booked a room at the Habitat Suite Hotel, the only hotel I found that accommodated chemically sensitive individuals.

* * *

Three days later, Amtrak pulled into Austin's station on a misty February nineteenth, 2011. I checked into the Habitat Suites

Hotel and called the relocation realtor, Lesa, to help me look for a non-toxic place to live. I pulled out my laptop and got busy finishing the editing on three books I started in New Mexico: *Kate's Way*, *The Basket Weaver*, and *Voices from the Land*. Like you, Mom, I never do one creative project at a time. I near drove my book designer crazy. She lived in Santa Fe, and at one point we were doing four books and two booklets at the same time! During those first few days in the hotel, I also applied for my Texas counseling license and sought out a writing community so I could find people with like interests. From the first night in the hotel, I worked to get my life organized. I was fed up with chaos. I had to find a way to make money, make connections, and find a home, again. I knew this pattern well and had lost count of how many cycles I had lived through.

Lesa found a place with tile and wood floors. I signed the lease and called the moving company to send my few possessions. This was a far cry from the spacious landscape I had fallen in love with in the past six years. A Holiday Inn was the view from my bedroom, and several freeways merged high above the ground. Large poles shot into the air replete with silver cables going in all directions. My computer faced a brick wall, not the Santa Fe Mountains or acres of buffalo grass, and bushes against my window were pruned into oppression, not the unadulterated landscape of tumbleweeds and hundred-year-old trees. I hardly recognized my life. But I did recognize the scene in front of me as the vision I had before I left New Mexico. Such clairvoyant and strange events I could only share with you, Mom. I knew you would understand.

I couldn't get my private practice started quickly enough because the vetting process with insurance companies usually takes two years. I wanted to enroll in UT's writing program, but I wasn't sure I could financially survive if I did. I decided I could manage the move except for one unexpected thing: compound

PTSD due to the awakened trauma from the events in California combined with the personal thefts, betrayals, house invasions, and financial matters forcing me to close my shop, sell my beloved home and land. I tried to write what I was feeling but I couldn't. It scared me. I had no one to call for help, nor did I have anyone to come over and make sure I was okay. I did what I could. I began writing words, simple drops of words on a page in my journal. If that was all I could do, then that was what I was going to do. Eventually I turned those words to phrases and soon I was writing verses. I wound up self-publishing two books of poetry. If I was going to suffer; I was going to make it pay. Beauty for ashes became my new motto.

The condo Lesa found bordered a beautiful neighborhood. I went in search of a church I could walk to on Sunday mornings. Although I could not find an actual church building, the Holiday Inn had a sign outside advertising a new church starting in one of the conference rooms. I walked in and attended regularly. I made sure to meet the pastor and introduce myself to the congregants in case I needed help. I was ready for more of a community feeling.

A few weeks later I went to move a box of books and twisted my back. I was in excruciating pain and could barely drive, but I managed to turn on the computer and find a chiropractor a few miles from the condo. The area was unfamiliar to me, and driving through dense traffic in intense pain was scary, but I finally arrived at the office. The chiropractor tried to treat me, even trying acupuncture, but I screamed in agony. He called a cab and had the driver take me to the hospital where I waited ninety minutes with no one checking on me. By the time the doctor arrived I was ready to pass out from pain. I explained I was sensitive to chemical medications and asked if he would give me a light pain pill, nothing too strong. Without even looking at or speaking to me he wrote out a prescription and walked away. I complained to a nurse who witnessed the scene. "Is this how Austin hospitals work?" She just looked down and started working on her computer.

The chiropractor had called my pastor, who arrived at the hospital to drive me home, get my prescription, and pick up my car still at the doctor's office. He and his associate pastor tucked me into bed and left. Surprisingly I found that church where a church usually isn't—The Holiday Inn.

I had no food and couldn't get to the kitchen. I grabbed a handful of water as I passed the bathroom sink. I called a member of the church and told her my situation. I asked if she could bring me several dishes from an Italian restaurant. I figured I could eat cold spaghetti if I could get my body out of bed to open the refrigerator door. An hour later she was knocking at my door with several dinners.

The pain pills knocked me out for two weeks. After I finished the prescription, I found my mood rising and falling with no precipitating factors. No wonder people get addicted and crazy from pain meds.

Once I could get up and dressed, I had to look for work and go grocery shopping. I needed rest, but time was moving on, I didn't know how long it would take to find work, and my money from the sale of my home was running out. Time was of the essence. I knew I was suffering from chronic PTSD, but I had to push myself just the same. I could barely think about what I wanted for dinner. It scared me. I felt eager and ready, but my mind was still somewhere else, absorbing all the things that had come at me unceasingly. Here I was in another city, an ugly place from where I once sat, being forced to start again.

I had to stop looking backwards at all that was lost and done to me, but it wasn't easy. Those events kept a heavy cloak of grief and fear over me, and as hard as I tried, I couldn't shake it.

It seemed like a good idea to use my marketable skills while waiting to get vetted by the insurance companies to start my private practice. I searched for legal secretary jobs, but things had changed since I started working as a legal secretary. I couldn't get a job without a paralegal degree. It would have cost me thousands of dollars and taken almost two years. I couldn't believe it. I didn't have that much time; I needed something immediately.

I decided to "hit the pavement," as we used to call looking for work, driving into business centers to find whatever work I could. In case you were wondering, there is no more pavements. Receptionists wouldn't even look or talk to me. They handed me business cards with websites and told me to go online and fill out their forms. At sixty-three, with decades of experience, finding a job should have been easier. I drove up and down Austin applying for work. When I managed to get an interview, I was interviewed by women in their late twenties. One of them asked me where I wanted to be in my career in thirty years.

I called an organization for those over fifty and got on their waiting list for employment, then applied for food stamps. I had planned to be retired by sixty-three, living on the beach, writing books, traveling. Instead, I was in Austin, a nightmare of concrete, trying not to panic. Eventually I got a call to go to work part-time for minimum wage. I loved the job and was good at it. Then one day I entered the coffee room to find a man with a respirator mask on his face and a canister on his back. He was spraying pesticides along the walls. My desk was by the coffee room, and every day I heard employees complain about being sick. I called the organization that placed me and asked if they would send me to another company.

I met with the supervisor and two other women to discuss my options. One of the women told me I was too sick to work in buildings and she didn't want to help me find a job. She said helping me was too much work. Too sick? I was not going to settle for that description after all I had been through. I told her no one was going to tell me I was too sick and told her not to speak about sickness around me. I hadn't healed as much as I had by telling myself I was sick. I told myself every day that I was doing well and getting better. Was my health still challenged? Yes. Was I getting better? Yes. The body listens. People who tell themselves they are sick feel sick. So why would I do that?

I told the cynical woman Austin is a big town, and I will fit in somewhere. She continued talking negative about me and my situation. I put my hands over my ears to drown her out and told the director sitting in front of me that I would not listen to her assertion that I was too sick to work.

He stared at me for quite a while. I couldn't figure out how he was processing this conversation. I stared back, my eyes unblinking. I called the shots when it came to my health; I earned that right. I didn't care how strange I looked or sounded; I was not backing down. With all I had been through and the nearly million dollars I had spent on my health and dozens of moves, I was going to leave there with a job interview, or I wasn't going to leave.

The director had a stack of wellness and good food videos on the corner of his desk. I figured that was a good sign he would see my point. Mom, you taught me how to break the myths of how women should behave when someone wants to hold them back. You would have been proud of me. I was not going to walk away with my tail between my legs. Every step of the last eleven years had been a challenge, and I was not going to back down now.

The supervisor finally reached into his drawer and brought out a map of Austin, which he opened over all the files on his desk. He asked me where I lived and how far I was willing to travel from home. He circled the area with a red pen then told the two women sitting on the side of the room with blank faces to find companies within that radius. Twenty-minutes later, I left the office with two numbers to call. I drove home in celebratory tears.

I had to drive across Austin for the interviews because they were at opposite ends from each other. The next day, someone from the placement organization called. Both employers wanted to hire me. I chose the position in the heart of Austin because it was a counseling-related intake job.

Shortly after I was hired, the firm hired an Army veteran. I recognized the minute he walked through the door that he had PTSD. He assaulted me one day on the way to the coffee room. I asked the administration to help because he continued giving me a difficult time. Instead of caring about their responsibility for safety in the workplace, they retaliated against me, and I was terminated.

I used to teach supervisors how to handle harassment, and I tried to teach them how to manage the situation and what their legal responsibility was. Imagine, Mom, I'm teaching lawyers how to handle an assault in the workplace. However, they decided it was much easier to let me go than to confront the veteran. I was escorted out of the office as if I had committed a crime.

About a month later a woman I met in the counseling field emailed me. Without knowing what had just happened, she told me she needed an LCSW to present a two-hour workshop for therapists on how to deal with a bully in the workplace. She wanted to know if I was interested. I couldn't email her fast enough. YES! I prepared my presentation, then called an employment attorney to find out if California law and Texas law were the same since it was in California that I taught harassment in the workplace. I gave my situation to the attorney as a hypothetical example to see if he could recommend legal cases to research. I thought the more resources I had, the better my presentation would be. He asked if this was my story, and I confessed it was. I had two months left before the statute of limitations ran out, and he thought I had a case. I met with him and sued.

I won. The money I got from the suit was just enough to hire a marketing agency to teach me how to set up an online website to help authors sell their books. I called and told them I had been assaulted by another worker. The woman who answered the phone was the same woman who didn't want to find me a job because she said I was too sick.

Her response was, "These things happen."

"Not to me," I said and hung up.

Eventually I wrote a small manual entitled, *How to Deal with a Bully in the Workplace.* Beauty from the ashes!

Still unable to find full time work, I began teaching writing classes online for an international writing group for women. I was not surprised when my students said writing about trauma had helped them overcome long-term and pervasive PTSD symptoms. They asked how I knew writing helped with PTSD. I explained I had been through PTSD in my own life, and that writing had helped me get through it. Did I have to go through all the trauma in the last eleven years to help others? I don't know. The more hard times I lived through, it seemed, the less I knew about anything.

The Bible says God's ways are not our ways, and His understanding is not man's. I didn't have to understand any of it, and it was a good thing, because I didn't. My plans for my life were not these.

SIXTY-THREE

Let's move on to January 2013, Mom. I think this is one of those stories you will love the most. I hope by now you understand I have seen God's hand in my life and that this soliloquy in book form is to thank you for insisting I go to church every Sunday and reinforcing we have a God who loves us. Believing in God didn't seem to serve me then, just like math didn't seem to serve me in the fourth grade.

Had it not been for the scriptures in the Bible I suspect I would have become hard-hearted, unforgiving, and mean. It was difficult to take the higher road when I was suffering at the hands of others, some I trusted, some I loved, some didn't have a substantial relationship with me at all, yet many dug their fingers into my life in harmful ways just the same.

I had lived in the Austin condo for two years when I got a note saying the owner wanted to sell. I called Lesa and she helped me find another apartment. Before I moved in, I asked the manager if there had been any leaks in the apartment because I had dealt with enough water damage in the last decade to last a million lifetimes. She said there hadn't been any leaks, so I signed the lease.

The first night I moved in, it rained, and while I was on the phone with a friend I noticed water running down the plastic slats of my blinds and streaking the walls. For five years I tried to get management to fix the leaks. No one thought the issue with leaks was of high priority, so my maintenance request was delegated to the back of the line.

It was January, and my account had dropped to only $3,000. Clients were not calling yet and the insurance companies were taking their sweet time in vetting me. I tried to remain calm and focused. One night I opened my Bible and read about the power of tithing. I went to my desk, wrote a small check, sent it to one of the ministries I listened to each morning, then waited. I'm sure you are laughing at this, Mom because you know that of all my virtues, patience is not even on the list.

In February I sent another check. I told God I would sit at my desk, in faith, waiting until He answered my call for clients. I told Him I was knocking, asking for, and seeking his help. That's what the Bible told me to do, so that's what I was doing. I did not see tithing as a test of my faith or proof that I was finally learning patience. No, I saw it as nothing short of having my skin peeled off one epidermal cell at a time. It was difficult to send money when I needed money. It seemed irrational and irresponsible, but I did it anyway, in faith, because the Bible made it clear to tithe.

March came, no clients. I sent another tithe. I told God I was not giving up. I was willing to tithe away as much money as I had because the Bible says faith is hope in the unseen, and I was hoping to the best of my ability. That childhood memory of standing on the corner wondering if I had enough faith for my life was again returning. I decided the answer was an astounding, yet slightly wavering, "yes." I stopped paying attention to that judgmental part of me. I stopped listening to the unknowing voices of those around me. *This is soul work,* I told myself, *and I am going to continue waiting.*

March fifteenth brought one call from a new client. By the end of the month, I had eight clients, nearly a part-time practice.

Month after month my practice built up. I kept getting calls, and within the year I was seeing twenty clients a week. Caller after caller told me they were drawn to my profile on PsychologyToday. com. They told me they weren't sure why, but they knew I could help them.

Slowly, my life began to recover. Then September, 2017 brought Hurricane Harvey. It was fierce. Rain pelted the ground until the water rushed down the small hill into the apartment attached to mine, flowing through that apartment into my kitchen. I got up at two in the morning to get a drink of water and my wool kitchen rug was floating like Aladdin's carpet two feet above the floor. I ran to my neighbor's apartment with my wet vac and banged on his door. If you can picture this, Mom, he comes to his door in his underwear, standing in two feet of water, his dog barking. The wind was blowing so hard while I tried to talk to him I could barely stand upright. He let me inside to vacuum the water in his apartment. Then he took his dog and left to go stay at his girlfriend's place while I removed the water from his place. Once I finished draining his apartment, I ran to mine. But the storm hadn't ended, and another flood of water poured into his apartment and through the wall into mine.

Water also streamed down my walls evidenced by soaking sheetrock. I called maintenance. The manager did not want to hear it. In the morning, she told me she was too busy with other crises. Long story short, I lost another full household due to the accumulation of mold spores from inside the walls. Renter's insurance did not reimburse for mold. It takes mold twenty-four to forty-eight hours to become dangerous to breathe, and once it contacts your belongings, they become trash. My apartment in shambles, I tried to pack as much as I could, knowing I wouldn't be able to save much. There was some hope for items I could put in the washer, dryer, or dishwasher. I was numb.

This was my seventh full household loss. The Bible uses

numbers a lot, and seven is the number of completion. I was counting on it.

Again, I remembered that voice and its message:

There's always more!
There's always more!

I sat in the main lobby of the leasing office crying, refusing to leave. I was not going to be homeless again. They didn't want to stop the projects they were working on to attend to me. I insisted. One office worker made fun of me because I was crying. I ignored her. I was right and I knew it. I was under their lease. I belonged to them. They had to put me somewhere.

I spoke to one of the maintenance crew and told him to break through my wall to confirm the water for himself. The manager instructed him not to break through the wall, but I insisted, or I was going to do it myself. An office run by girls under twenty-five who never owned a house and never saw what mold could do was not going to dictate this matter. This particular maintenance man had worked in my apartment many times, so he knew me and trusted me. He broke through my wall and examined it with a moisture meter. The wall was soaked, and he could see water streaming in from above. Mold was already damaging the walls. He realized the water was coming from the building next door, traveling across the walkway and draining into my apartment. He pressured the manager to take my case seriously. Reluctantly, they put me in another apartment.

What an amazing apartment it was. It overlooked the greenbelt with hundreds, maybe thousands, of elms, cedar, and other nameless trees. I stared into the canyon, stunned by its beauty. Instead of a dusty, noisy parking lot, I was now staring into a forest. I had a white kitchen, not like the one I remodeled in California, but white, and with pantry space. The closets had built-in closet organizers. This was an apartment I could decorate to look like a home.

SEVENTY-ONE

Until this point, Austin's winters had been mild. In 2011, all I needed was a heavy sweater or light jacket. It was a pleasant surprise after the heavy snowfalls in Santa Fe. But in February, 2021, Austin had a horrible ice storm, and I lost electricity. The temperature inside my apartment was forty degrees in the daytime and colder at night. I had no way to cook or stay warm. And, as if that week wasn't difficult enough, Valentine's Day was the fourteenth, the day you died was the fifteenth, and your birthday was the seventeenth. That was an overwhelming week of grief.

It was Sunday night when I lost power, and by Tuesday I knew I had to get out of the apartment and find a warm place or I would need medical help. Icicles eight inches long draped along my wrought iron fence. The greenbelt in front of me looked like the stalactite crystals in caves. The ground around the apartments and driveway were slick enough for ice skates. Cars spun in snake-like motions on the roads because most Austinites don't know how to operate a car in snow, let alone on ice. Some neighbors didn't even own gloves and tried to dig out their vehicles using dust pans and table salt; some used their bare fingers to pull snow away from their cars' tires. You would have found that quite amusing, Mom.

There weren't enough wool blankets to take the bite out of

the frigid air. I had eight layers of wool blankets wrapped around my shoulders and still trembled. My only food was a handful of raw almonds and pistachio nuts. I layered my bed with twelve blankets and climbed under them hoping to get a good night's rest, but to no avail. It's not possible to sleep while shivering.

Had I had ice skates, I could have made a fun time of it and skated to a warm hotel. The mail, supposed to be delivered in any kind of weather, did not come. Austin had no preparation for such weather. Cars that spun out on highways and streets were abandoned; people walked off freeways to try and make it home.

The next day, most of my neighbors were packed and heading out to the main road to wait for family or friends who had four-wheel-drive trucks to rescue them. I stood in the parking lot wondering how I was going to get out, or if I could sustain another night at home. How long would it be before our power came back, and who did I know who could come get me?

The COVID pandemic was still quite active at the time. The police said they would drive me to a shelter an hour away, but they wouldn't take me to a friend's house ten minutes down the road, where I had no risk of getting COVID. It made no sense. I wasn't going to a shelter with dozens of people and run the risk of getting COVID. I was in my seventies, Mom, and older people were dying at a rapid pace from this pandemic.

I walked into my kitchen and shouted prayers for help. My prayers have always been an internal, sacred action. I've held them close to my heart in reverence, and yet here I was shouting at my ceiling. As my fear for my life heightened, so did my boldness. I prayed someone would come to my door and rescue me, but no one came. I'd put on my heavy boots, go out, knock on doors for help. No one answered. I'd go back to my apartment, take off my heavy snow boots, gather some energy, and try again. I was wearing myself out.

A quick, hard knock at my door brought some hope. One of my neighbors wanted to know if I had dog food. They were leaving to stay with friends but had no dog food to take. I had no dog, so I had no food, but I did have a bag of doggie treats I gave to their dogs on my daily walks. I was about to ask him if he could take me with him, but he was gone before I knew it.

I turned on my battery radio but couldn't get the weather report, not that I needed anyone to tell me how serious this was. The apartment complex was nearly empty.

Daylight was waning, and the sun was nearing the horizon. It would be even colder soon. I called another friend in full panic. I told her there was nowhere I could go, and I was really scared. She ran different scenarios of places I could go, not fully realizing the situation because she and her husband had power and were cozying up close to their fireplace. I kept explaining I had no way to get to any of the places she recommended. Dare I invite myself into their snuggly situation? It finally registered how bad it was, and I heard her ask her husband if I could go to their house. Did she need his permission to help a friend in such a dire situation? He agreed, but I had no way to get there. She gave me the numbers for Uber and a taxi service. They weren't sending anyone out, especially since the daylight was almost gone.

She told me to pack a suitcase for a week and find a way. I ran to my closet and threw some clothes in an overnight bag. With deepening resolve, I pulled on my snow boots for the umpteenth time and ran back out to the driveway in search of help. Out of 400 apartments *someone* had to be able to help me. I was unwilling to give up, especially now that I had a place to stay.

As I walked onto the driveway, a man walked out of the woods carrying a cardboard box filled with tree branches for his fireplace. I asked him if he wanted to make a hundred dollars. He asked me what I needed. I told him I needed a ride just fifteen minutes away. He said his wife was having contractions, but he would ask her. I asked him what kind of car he had, and he pointed to a small Kia.

"Forget it," I said. "That car won't get out of the driveway. Attend to your wife."

I went back to my apartment discouraged, struggled to take off my snow boots, then revved up my fury and determination and found the force to head out again. I knocked on all the doors, everyone had left. I looked around the parking lot. Most of the cars were snowed in. There was a large black truck in front of one of the apartments and I walked carefully on ice to its front door and knocked. A man opened the door.

"Is that your truck?" I asked.

The man ran out, thinking someone had hit it. I explained I needed a ride just fifteen minutes away and would pay him a hundred dollars. I thought his truck might make it down highway 360. His wife came out of the apartment dressed in an apron with a wooden spoon in her hand. They had a fire blazing in their fireplace. She called her husband back and abruptly told me the weather was too bad and he wasn't going anywhere. Then she shut the door in my face.

I went back to my apartment and called my friend. "I can't get anyone to give me a ride. I know I won't make it through the night in this apartment. It is freezing here. I can't take it. I'm very cold."

There didn't seem to be a way to turn this situation around. I turned the lock on my door, feeling defeated, then heard Pastor Kenneth Copeland's words: "Speak boldly to God." I began another round of shouting prayers towards my ceiling.

"You told me you wouldn't leave me nor forsake me. You
promised me your help. You promised me if I asked you,
if I knocked, you would answer, and I am asking, I am

knocking, send someone to get me out of here."

I shouted and I shouted. I shouted Bible scriptures. I was surprised at how many I remembered.

"God, you said, 'fear not for you are with me.' You said you would not leave me. You said you would protect me in Psalm ninety-one. You said to ask, so I am asking. God, you have pulled me through many home disasters, two years of homelessness, a paralyzing illness that nearly killed me. I will not die in this apartment. I am boldly asking, 'Will you help me now, again?'"

After I laid out my temper tantrum on the Lord, I found a surge of inner strength that pushed me to struggle into my boots one more time. I ran out to the driveway not knowing what I was going to do or what would make this time any different. Darkness was seconds away. My options were grim.

I trudged to the driveway. I was exhausted and my desperation was unmanageable. In the middle of the driveway stood a gold, damaged Camry. My rational mind said, *this car won't make it to the corner on dry concrete let alone on a slick layer of ice.* What options did I have? I knocked on the window with force. A young woman in her late twenties looked up from her lap and asked me what I needed.

"How would you like to make a hundred bucks?" I asked.

"What do you need?" she replied with a wide smile. I was stunned at her lack of distress.

"I need a ride." I said, the cold air catching my breath.

"Sure," she said in a singsong voice, sweet and positive. "Hop in."

"Really?"

"Sure, hop in."

"I have a suitcase packed. I'll be right back."

I walked quickly and carefully back to my apartment, grabbed my suitcase, and went to lock my door, aware of the fading light and the danger this woman was putting herself in for me. I struggled to find my house key. I knew it was on the key ring but I couldn't find it. I panicked. After three or four spins around the ring, I located it, locked my door, and, trying to manage the heavy suitcase while walking on ice with the hundred-dollar bill tucked in my hand, I reached her car. I got in, pulled the door shut, then broke out crying. "I can't stay here. It is too cold. I can already feel my body giving out. Thank you so very much."

"It's all good," she said.

She reassured me she would take me wherever it was I needed to go. Fortunately, I remembered to put my address book on top of my suitcase. Why I even took it I had no idea. I knew where my friend lived. She took the book and found my friend's house number for her GPS. She took a minute to type it in as I anxiously reminded her the sun had seconds before it was fully past the horizon, and we would be in the dark. I told her we had better get going.

"All's good," she reminded me again.

Slowly she drove out of the complex and started down the icy street, negotiating its slightly hilly terrain. Cars were skidding, turning in circles, or abandoned. I was praying we wouldn't hit one of them, but the young woman handled her car with great adeptness.

The road had a dip in the middle I had never noticed before. I panicked, fearing we would have to turn around, or worse, leave the car and walk back up the hill to our apartments.

"Not to worry," she reinforced.

She didn't seem to have a care in the world. She tried again to make it up the dip in the road. We couldn't get enough traction even after the third try. Suddenly, I remembered there was another way. I told her we could go another way if she could back up the street and turn to the right. I told her I couldn't remember the name of the street but if I saw it, I would know it. The sun had just fully descended. Her ability to be so relaxed was starting to grate on me. *Why isn't she upset about the matter? Can't she see the predicament we're in?*

She introduced herself as Elizabeth as calmly as if we were at a café. She told me she had been driving on ice all day to help her brother who had just moved to Austin from Nebraska. She said she knew nothing about Austin, but she drove on ice all the time back home and knew what she was doing. I was stunned by her grace, good spirits, and lack of anxiety. It felt like I was living in an episode of *Touched by an Angel*. I tried to take a deep breath but couldn't. All I could do was choke on my fear that we would get stuck along the way, and then what? It was quite dark, and soon it would be darker.

I could feel PTSD symptoms begin to take over my nervous system. I had had too many experiences in which I had to abruptly leave my home. A heavy shadow of dread formed around me. I tried to stay in the moment and not get sucked into the past. I was wrestling with my own mind.

Elizabeth drove at a consistent speed under twenty miles an hour. We got down hills and turned corners seamlessly; it seemed I was riding on a cloud. We passed large trucks stranded on ice on Jollyville Road and small cars spinning. How she was managing I couldn't explain; we passed them all effortlessly. Some street signs were lit, but most weren't. We had one steeper hill to go before we got to Highway 360 and I warned her it was treacherous in the rain, let alone on ice. Her mood and emotional temperament remained cheerful, positive, and unaffected by the situation. We got to the bottom of the hill, sometimes veering onto small patches of snow to keep traction. She kept reminding me she was from Nebraska and did this all the time.

All the highway lights were out except one, and when we got to it, it turned red. I looked around. There were no cars.

"Don't stop," I said, "or we'll never get started again."

"No problem," she reassured me.

We drove slowly through the red light. What normally takes twelve to fifteen minutes took us approximately forty-five.

When we arrived at my friend's house I was still shaking. I handed Elizabeth the hundred-dollar bill, which she didn't want to accept. I stuck it in her cup holder.

"I probably owe you breakfast, lunch, and dinner for the rest of your life," I joked.

I told her I was worried about her getting home safely, but she reassured me she would be all right, and if she got stuck, she knew two guys with big trucks who would come to rescue her. Her smile never ceased. I walked across the icy road to my friend's house, my overnight bag pulling my shoulder down. I rang their doorbell, suddenly realizing I hadn't called to confirm I was coming. When the door opened, I collapsed into their arms.

It took five days for the power to come on in my area. I shuddered imagining how I would have survived that long in freezing temperatures with no heat or warm food. I felt blessed. Unlike other residents, I did not come home to a broken pipe spewing water all over my possessions.

On May sixth, 2021, I saw Elizabeth drive into the parking lot. At first I didn't recognize her because she was in a different car. She was on the phone, so I waited for her to end her call.

"Aren't you Elizabeth?"

"I got another car."

I gave her a hug. "You were my angel," I said, and heard the words come back at me.

We each took a step back, staring at each other in

amazement because we had spoken the same statement in perfect synchronization.

"You saved me from dying in a freezing apartment," I reminded her. "I had to spend five days at my friend's house. I wouldn't have survived with no heat or warm food."

"No," she replied. "I had just spent all my money on a family matter and needed money. Just when I was wondering how I was going to get some quick, I heard a knock on my car window asking how I would like to make a hundred dollars. You saved me. *You* are *my* angel."

I never saw Elizabeth again.

Oh Mom, isn't that an amazing story? I think of Elizabeth often. How many people like her does anyone meet in a lifetime? I think of people like Mike, James, Lesa, each entering my life at just the right moment. There are dozens more stories I could tell you, Mom. I'm only picking out the ones that have been testaments, without question, that God is a living God. He answers prayers whether you shout at him, like in this situation, or sit quietly praying on the floor, like when I found what I needed in *The New York Times* in 1972.

I'd share stories about the men I was involved with, but when I look back on them now, none of them would have fit into my life. They all resisted change, and they either walked out after promising to marry me or I had to break up with them because they only thought of themselves. Not one of them wanted me to live my best life. They wanted a woman to make them look and feel important. Had I married any of them, I know that an important movement of my life would have been interrupted. Ironically, I used to believe men were the important relationships of my life and I was solely focused on finding the "right" man. Now they barely hold space in this narrative, not because my relationships with them didn't play an important role, but because the movement of my own life became larger and of more significance.

In one relationship I got to experience what it was like to be a mom. I loved it and I loved that little six-year-old boy. We had become quite close snuggling on the couch as he shared his day and learning how to eat home-cooked meals instead of burritos from the corner gas station, teaching him how to cook and garden and work out some problems. When his father unexpectedly walked out with his little boy while I was at work, I thought I would never recover. It took three years to stabilize my life. Even my cat would wait at the door every other weekend looking depressed when he didn't show up. He told his son I had kicked them out. His father was a coward for lying and blaming me because his own fears of commitment got the better of him. And the man who ended our two-year relationship on the night of the blue moon in my favorite romantic restaurant, with Christmas songs in the background, how much space does he deserve? Or the man, again after being together two years, who told me at Thanksgiving he would give me a ring on Christmas but didn't, who walked out angry when I asked him about why he didn't give me a ring, scolding me with, "How could you do this to me?"

You were right, Mom. It takes two years to see if a man has the integrity to commit. Each of these relationships ended at the end of two years, and with each ending I thought of you.

But I must tell you about another prophetic dream before this conversation ends because it involves all the women in our family who put strength, determination, faith, and fortitude into my blood. I realize I am never far from any of you. Your souls live on in me, and for that I am grateful.

Get ready for this one, Mom because as hard as this one is to tell you, I know it must be told.

SEVENTY-TWO

In July, 2022, I had three dreams that woke me in the middle of the night. In each dream I was sitting in a small unadorned room in front of a doctor who announced with a stoic demeaner, "Jan, you have cancer." In each dream I had no reaction; I just stared at the doctor, then woke up.

I went on the computer to research dreams about cancer. I found articles that indicated fearful dreams of having cancer were common for people under high stress, and I was under stress. I was seeing clients from home because a pandemic was quickly spreading around the world, stopping life as we knew it. People were having their food delivered because going grocery shopping, or to church, or talking to the mail carrier threatened the possibility of contracting the deadly virus. Citizens were dying by the thousands, and hospitals and nurses were at their limit, working overtime while our president told us not to worry, it was like the flu and would magically leave.

Trying to avoid chemicals was bad enough. This was not just avoidance—it was full-on isolation. It was a dreadful experience. Not being able to see people smile or watch them speak changes the energy in human contact. It is a half-personal experience. Knowing these dreadful dreams could be a product of stress, I relaxed. It made perfect sense. Clients were more stressed and anxious than usual, why shouldn't I be as well?

A few nights later, I took a nice, hot shower and climbed into bed to do my usual reading. At seventy-two, I was thankful my health had improved and I had been able to stay in my apartment for years. My diet of primarily organic foods, use of non-toxic cleaning products, wearing organic and natural clothing, and daily exercise all seemed to pay off. Just as I was feeling full of gratitude for my life stabilizing and my health recovering, I got up to go to the bathroom and noticed an egg-sized circle of pus on my sheet. Within a half hour I was bleeding, seriously bleeding. I immediately called my doctor's nurse and went in the next day for a checkup. The doctor wanted to do a sonogram and probe. It showed water on my uterus. She suspected it was a polyp, which is cancerous only .014 percent of the time. I was told not to worry. I did my best with that request. I felt well, so I wasn't too worried, except for the dreams of cancer continuing.

After the sonogram and probe, the doctor said she wanted to remove any polyps and learn more about what the sonogram was showing. A week later I had the biopsy. One of my writing friends, Ati, stayed with me overnight in case I started bleeding and had to be taken to the hospital. I had no separate room for her in my apartment, so she had to sleep on the floor. Like you, Mom, I enjoy being an accommodating hostess, but Ati and I managed with the little I could offer in a one bedroom apartment.

The doctor said she would call in a few days with the results. I wasn't worried. I thought I was just going through the procedure to make sure nothing was wrong. The day after the biopsy, the doctor called. I told her I felt great and was glad it was over, but I was still bleeding quite heavily. I was scheduled to start seeing clients on telehealth and was eager to move on. The doctor hesitated, then quietly and slowly said she found something in the sample. Two small patches she scraped off my uterus were endometrial cancer. *Cancer?*

If there is ever one single word to stop your world and drop you into hell, it's cancer. And whoever says words don't matter hasn't had that word spoken to them. I lost my breath, then heard myself ask, "Am I going to die?" I did not feel the words come out of my mouth. I did not feel the phone in my hand.

She listened as I repeated it couldn't be true because I felt great. When I was finished spinning and denying, she gave me a referral to an oncologist and told me to call her right away. *Right away?*

How I got through seeing clients that morning I cannot explain. I took on the usual posture of being a therapist and walked through my day. I can honestly say I didn't remember much.

I asked God how I could be so sick and still feel so strong and healthy? I sat still and this is what I heard:

"I made you strong so you can handle this."

What? Really?

God doesn't make people sick. I do not believe that. God is a healer, but I knew better than to challenge that message. I knocked on my neighbor's door. I had to talk to someone. I didn't know her very well, even though she had lived across from me for a couple of years. I told her the diagnosis was endometrial cancer. She invited me inside to sit and talk. I didn't know she was an oncology nurse until she knew just what to say when I didn't even know what to ask.

I do not believe in luck, and I do not believe anything is random. How to explain this diagnosis after decades of working to maintain good health? I felt like air. I felt lost.

I set up an oncology appointment and called friends to see if anyone could take me. No one could. Someone recommended I try an online neighborhood watch community. I felt pathetic putting out a local bulletin to strangers in the community for help, but what choice did I have? I knew I'd be preoccupied and too nervous to drive myself to the doctor's office. I posted that

I needed someone to take me to the oncology appointment, figuring no one would put themselves into such a dramatic situation, and forgot about it.

As my appointment approached, I decided to see if anyone responded. I couldn't believe what I saw. I had a dozen women offering to take me to the appointment. Many of them had gone through the same thing or had dealt with a friend or parent who did. Such brave women. I felt quite blessed and relieved. Sometimes strangers can be more supportive than the people you think love and care for you.

Turns out I needed a radical hysterectomy. Again, I had to find someone to stay with me the night after the surgery. Jeanne, one of the women in my writers' group offered to help. I started planning how to take care of her while she stayed with me, but she stopped me. "I've got this," she kept saying. "I've got this."

And she did. She really did. I didn't have to think about anything. She picked me up at five in the morning the day of the surgery and scrubbed me down with antiseptic wipes. There was no nurse to do it, and I couldn't figure out which wipe went where, I was trembling so much from fear. When I couldn't wake up from the anesthesia they had to keep me overnight. Still, Jeanne did not give up helping me. She returned the next morning and waited until they got me ready to be discharged. She spent two days hanging around to see how she could help, sleeping on my floor, making me tea, making sure I ate.

The doctor had successfully removed the cancer, so I didn't need chemotherapy or radiation, but she insisted I take nine weeks medical leave after the surgery. I tried to whittle her down in time because I didn't want to stop treatment with my clients, but no matter how I negotiated with her, she kept repeating I needed nine weeks. And she was right. I spent the first four weeks in bed, then I was able to start walking to the mailbox and being on my feet long enough to scramble an egg. I read nineteen books in nine weeks. I took it slow because doing any activity that used my core was dangerous.

The week before my birthday I went back to work. If there is anything to take the complaining out of you, Mom, it's a life of repeated events that threaten your ability to take care of yourself. I thought about how sick you got from your incessant smoking and wondered how you let your strength be taken by it. I'll never know what it was like for you. I think about it a lot, more than you would think. You were my rock. I know we had turbulent times, but love can overlook them. I think what was really between us was your expectation that I would give up making my own decisions for my life and continue to let you make them. You wanted to plan my marriage to men you chose and have me be there for you when you were in need. You refused to accept I could make my own decisions and follow the dreams in my heart.

You didn't want me to grow up and be on my own, but how could I grow up and not be on my own? That didn't make sense. I realize you never recovered from Grandma's death, and on some level I haven't recovered from yours. I guess this narrative is an effort to do that, not to let you go, but to make peace. I just want peace with it all, Mom. I just want peace.

I wrote a poem about the strength I needed and put framed photos of all the women in my family around my bedroom. They reminded me how strong you all were, and because I was part of you, I was strong too.

HISTORY

Wind bites rocks and they take it.
Darkness swallows day and it takes it.
The full moon as witness.

Life slaps at me.
I'm not as strong as the rock or the day.
The moon as my witness.
Some challenges seem
unmanageable.

Nana, I wonder, at 16
in the early 1900s
how did you manage after arriving at Ellis Island
knowing no English
not being able to read or write?
How did you manage?

Grandma, I wonder, at 29
in the 1920s
how did you manage
the betrayal of the father of your
two children
one still in the womb while
raising your
four nieces and nephews as well?
How did you manage?

Great grandma, I wonder, at 18
in the late 1880s
how did you manage
married life at only 18
cooking for 18 farms hands?
How did you manage?

Mom, I wonder, at 18
in the early 1940s
how did you manage

the oppression of women
that stole your dream to
become a scientist?
How did you manage?

Photos of these strong women sit
on a table near my bed
reminding me that I too
can manage
a diagnosis of cancer.
All of you,
you are my mountains of strength
breathing in my blood.
You can do it
You can do anything, I hear them chant.

You are us.

We are you!

You can manage!

SEVENTY-FOUR

In 2023, I went to a three-day writer's retreat. At this workshop, the facilitator led us through a meditation in which we were to imagine ourselves as the mythological daughter of the goddess Demeter, whose name was Persephone. We were instructed to descend to Hades, the god of darkness. Demeter was the goddess of agriculture. As Persephone descended into the depths of darkness to meet her love, Hades, her mother mourned for her daughter, refusing to eat or care for her crops.

As instructed, I imagined descending the spiral staircase towards Hades. The challenges of descending into the darkness felt like a knife peeling away my skin. Whatever was penetrating me on this rough journey cut through to my core and cut away all I didn't need with force and pressure. On this journey towards the depths, I felt pure solitude and experienced losses in all directions. There was nothing around me to sustain my life.

"What's next?" the facilitator asked.

I experienced a oneness of diving into my own core, then a oneness in meeting God. Through this meeting, I was recreating my relationship with you because I went nowhere without your essence inside me. This journey also emboldened an inner feminine divine. That was the answer I got. The essence was not just me, not just my feminine, but the feminine essence of all the daughters before me.

The facilitator asked: "Where are you?"

I looked around. I was in the woods with wildflowers by a rill. The birds were plentiful, and I saw an opening horizon. I embraced all the beauty around me. I didn't want to get sucked into the darkness of Hades. Hades had great evil and dark power, and it would have been easy to get sucked into his darkness and confusion. I fought Hades' pull and resisted falling into its futility but found and entered a dark part of the soul of the daughter. I continued to proceed down a spiral staircase. There was a large cavern before me, the cavern of Hades. At the bottom of the staircase, I faced an altar with these items on it:

small wooden cross
pen
scroll
pleasant hearty scent of musk

I heard Hades ask for a spiritual language to share with him. I kept my eyes on the cross and pen and scroll. At first, I thought the cross represented Jesus, but then I realized it was all the heavy-hearted parts of my own life, the cross I was bearing.

"What makes you feel pregnant with soul?" the facilitator called out.

My heart longed for the love of the Divine's self-expression, my self-expression, the want of it all swelled inside me. I wanted to know who I was.

The three objects on the altar stirred a heavy hunger to become one with all my complicated parts. To find an inner union, to fulfill deep longings raging in my soul where nothing is lacking, to make beauty from ashes, to make all the trials in my many challenges pay with the abundance of beauty through overcoming.

The object of these symbols was a gift, the pure energy of

being a daughter. All mothers are daughters.

I am that I am. That is the constant energy within. I love it beyond measure for it is fully me and I am fully it—I reclaimed this divineness as mine. I am an unquestionable, non-challenging, non-negotiable wholeness.

The facilitator calls out, "Describe the cavern."

It is a dark room with a lot of glittering gold and various trinkets. The cross, the pen, the scroll have their own language and that is to sing a song. They are my sound. They are my voice.

"How will you look after you ascend?" she asks.

I am wearing white, soft, gentle colors, some silver, nothing brazen. Right before I ascend, I am handed a package to unwrap. It is a new language—words carefully selected—only words that honor the self are inside the box, seducing me to create new threads of healing. I hold the box carefully and study its contents.

Hades takes a pomegranate and hands me three of its seeds with a directive that I put the three seeds in my mouth. He says I must return to him once a year for more soul work, to build a higher consciousness, a refining of the language of my divineness through our love for each other. This sacred sense of self can only be found in the darkness of solitude. Hades released me and I ascended to return to the mother, my mother.

Once ascended, I see my mother, and she now takes back her strength upon seeing me. All is good again. Finally, my forehead is kissed by sunshine, and I stand on earth with my gifts and the new language earned through entering the darkness of my soul. I hear deeply that nothing is wasted in life. Every feeling, scent, experience, struggle, failed love, it all matters. No piece can be removed.

I hold the pen and scroll, and I write my story so others know we all have a sacred story. No one can get into my pen without my permission. This is the holy expression of my soul, the mouth of my inner voice.

Let go to let come in.

* * *

In the myth of Demeter and her daughter Persephone, Demeter has become weak. She has sacrificed her strength for her daughter. She has allowed her crops to fail. Her life has lost its meaning without her beautiful daughter near her. Sound familiar, Mom?

The relationship daughters have with their mothers is the most enigmatic and powerful relationship they have with anyone. As long as daughters keep coming out of their mothers, there is no permanent independence from them. Like Demeter, mothers await the return of their daughters. And like Persephone, daughters want to return to the arms and hearts of their mothers, but not before they have found themselves. The search of daughters for that profound connection with themselves is universal, and I can't help but wonder why mothers don't realize this, as daughters are mirrors of them.

For now, that's all I wanted to share with you. Mostly, I wanted to thank you for showing me how to be strong, how to endure hard times, and I wanted to thank you for giving me the opportunity to know God, to teach me that having a spiritual foundation for my life is necessary.

I might never understand why our relationship broke as it did. Maybe it was a combination of unwanted experiences happening in your life and the heartbreaking experiences happening in mine. Maybe it was the archetype of mothers and daughters, and we were destined to share the journey no matter what we did.

I spent too much time being angry with you, and I wonder if you think you spent too much time being angry with me. Maybe what it's all about is replacing anger and fear with forgiveness and love.

I can truly say I still miss you. I miss the smells of your homemade tomato sauce, the sounds of pots and drawers opening in the kitchen early in the morning, the smell of coffee brewing, seeing you at the kitchen table smoking, or sitting in the dining room making plans for holiday meals. I miss watching you walk up the stairs, your eyes burning from the cold, winter weather and welcoming my friends who came for a visit with a table full of deli food. I miss you so much. I look at my fingers as I type this and they are your fingers—long, thin, lean, always making and creating.

The grief in my heart cannot be dissected. It is complicated and filled with many memories and losses, but most of all my heart is filled with love for you. So, I will keep this complication of emotions for now, just the way it is, because that is all I have left. That is my home where I will always find you. That, and The Green Tea Room.

Life will break you. Nobody can protect you from that, and living alone won't either, for solitude will also break you with its yearning. You have to love. You have to feel. It is the reason you are here on earth. You are here to risk your heart. You are here to be swallowed up. And when it happens that you are broken, or betrayed, or left, or hurt, or death brushes near, let yourself sit by an apple tree and listen to the apples falling all around you in heaps, wasting their sweetness. Tell yourself that you tasted as many as you could.

—LOUISE ERDRICH, *The Painted Drum*

ACKNOWLEDGMENT

I owe a deep gratitude to my writing mentors: Natalie Goldberg, Judyth Hill, Len Leatherwood, and Ellen Bass whose classes helped me keep my pen moving during this intense project.

To Mary Hall, editor, and Rich Carnahan, book designer, at Publish Pros, many thanks again for a job well done and for the support you continue to give my many writing projects.

During the writing of this book, I lost my dear friend Peter Gilhaney to a sudden heart attack. I cannot write about Brooklyn or my life without honoring Peter and our 66-year friendship. He was a steadfast root in my life, in addition to sharing our birthday. May each of you have such a treasured friend.

Also in my thoughts is my friend Charles Capone, who passed away after I moved to Austin.

ABOUT THE AUTHOR

Jan Marquart is a licensed clinical social worker, educator, author, writing instructor, and dynamic motivational speaker.

She has authored over two dozen books and has been published in local newspapers in New Mexico and California. She has received the National Self-Published Book Award for 2000 from *Writers Digest* for her memoir, *The Breath of Dawn, A Journey of Everyday Blessings,* and received the Editor's Choice Award from the International Library of Poetry for her poem, "Yesterday." In 2013, she won the Editor's Choice award from Story Circle Network for *The Mindful Writer, Still the Mind, Free the Pen.* In 2021 she won second place in a poetry contest for her poem, "Old Crone," sponsored by Story Circle Network.

Jan's poems, essays, stories, and creative non-fiction pieces have been published online at: www.everywritersresource. com. Poetry Victims, www.ladyinkmagazine.com, Solecisms, IndianaVoiceJournal.com, Scars Publications (Down in the Dirt), and many others.

Most writers have a niche in which they write. Jan enjoys trying her pen in all genres. Her muse is constantly dancing to different tunes, practicing different structures, challenging those structures, and finding the need to hear her voice in all of them.

Jan has taught writing classes for Life Learning Institute, an organization for people over 50, and Story Circle Network, an international women's writing circle.

Her blogs are:
www.freethepen.wordpress.com
www.awarelivingnow.blogspot.com

Her site is:
JanMarquartBooks.com

She can be reached at:
Jan_marquart@yahoo.com